"My Reader
My Fellow-Labourer"

"My Reader
My Fellow-Labourer"

A STUDY of ENGLISH ROMANTIC PROSE

JOHN R. NABHOLTZ

University of Missouri Press
Columbia, 1986

Library of Congress Cataloging-in-Publication Data

Nabholtz, John R.
"My reader my fellow-labourer".

Bibliography: p.
Includes index.
1. English prose literature — 19th century — History and
criticism.   2. Romanticism — England.   3. Authors
and readers.   4. English language — Style.   I. Title.
PR778.R65N3   1986   828'.708'09   85–20118
ISBN 0-8262-0491-0 (alk. paper)

∞ This paper meets the minimum requirements of
the American National Standard for Permanence of Paper
for Printed Library Materials, Z39.48, 1984.

For Martin J. Svaglic

PREFACE

The relatively modest size of this book indicates that it is *not* a comprehensive study of romantic prose expression. There is no exploration of the writings of such major figures as De Quincey, Leigh Hunt, or Southey; nor are examples of all the prose genres surveyed, most notably absent being historical writing, biography/autobiography, or the dialogue-form found in Landor's *Imaginary Conversations* and Southey's *Colloquies*. There is also no attempt to examine formally the varieties of prose style in these writers. Instead, this is the exploration of one aspect of a very large and complex body of material, namely, *the endeavor in some of the most original romantic prose to retrain the reader in his habits of responding to the text*. To be sure, every period in the long history of English prose has in one way or another sought to alter the reader's relation to the prose text. *"My Reader My Fellow-Labourer"* offers some examples of this attempt in the romantic period. The Introduction examines the romantics' own remarks about the nature of prose and their stated expectations of the reader; the chapters that follow with their close reading of selected texts are intended as the implementation and demonstration of these more theoretical concerns.

Parts of this study were originally published in two scholarly journals. Gratitude for permission to use this material, considerably revised in most cases, is due to *The Wordsworth Circle*, for parts of Chapters Three and Five; *Studies in English Literature*, for parts of Chapter Two. Thanks are also due to the British Library, and to Mrs. A. H. B. Coleridge and Mrs. Priscilla Coleridge Needham for gracious permission to use some unpublished Coleridge material in Chapter Five.

A number of teachers, colleagues, and friends have stimulated and encouraged in various ways my exploration of this material, though some of them may be reluctant to acknowledge their influence in the results. Special obligations are due to Stuart Tave, who introduced me to romantic prose; and to W. P. Albrecht, Sheila Bartle-Harrod, Marilyn Gaull, James A. Houck, David Locke, Thomas J. Mann, and William Rueckert. Finally, much of the manuscript was prepared during a year's leave of absence from teaching duties. I am grateful to Loyola University of Chicago for financial support during this period, with special thanks to John S. Shea, then Chair of the English Department, and Ronald E. Walker, Vice-President and Dean of Faculties. Thomas J. Bennett, Director of Research Services, arranged for the typing of the manuscript.

J. R. N.
October 1985

CONTENTS

1. INTRODUCTION

"[The] field [of prose] is at present almost uncultivated," Wordsworth wrote in 1816; "we have adroit living prose writers in abundance; but impassioned, eloquent, and powerful ones not any, at least that I am acquainted with. Our Prose taking it altogether, is a disgrace to the country."[1] Coleridge concurred with this sharp criticism of current modes of prose, significantly for their encouragement of passive and desultory reading ("the habit of seeking in books for an idle and barren amusement"), and traced the condition to several sources: "the worst effects of habitual novel reading,"[2] "a passion for the unconnected in the minds of Englishmen" precipitated by the very excellence of the *Spectator* papers,[3] and "the fashionable *Anglo-gallican* Taste" for a prose of short sentences linked by no development of thought or even syntactical connection.[4] These culminated in an "obsti-

1. Letter of 11 March to John Scott, *The Letters of William and Dorothy Wordsworth: The Middle Years*, vol. 2, 285. Wordsworth nervously penned the following "P.S." to his letter:
I fear what I have said on Prose as now produced, may be misunderstood. Charles Lamb, my friend, writes prose exquisitely; Coleridge also has produced noble passages, so has Southey. But I mean that there is no body, of philosophical, impassioned, eloquent, finished prose now produced.
2. *The Friend*, ed. Barbara E. Rooke, in *The Collected Works of Samuel Taylor Coleridge*, vol. 4, ii, 11, 150.
3. *Collected Letters of Samuel Taylor Coleridge*, ed. Earl Leslie Griggs, vol. 3, 279. See also his remark about the difference between *The Friend* and *The Spectator* in *The Friend*, ii, 19.
4. *The Friend*, ii, 150. For additional references to *style coupé* and its deleterious effects, see *Letters of Coleridge*, vol. 2, 1179; vol. 3, 234, 237, 254, 282; *The Notebooks of Samuel Taylor Coleridge*, ed. Kathleen Coburn, entries 1759 (December 1803) and 3504 (April-July 1809); Lecture 14 "On Style" (13 March 1818), in *Coleridge's Miscellaneous Criticism*, ed. T. M. Raysor, p. 217.

nate . . . aversion to all intellectual effort . . . , the Queen Bee in the Hive of our errors and misfortunes, both private and national."[5]

De Quincey similarly objected to the "penury of thinking" induced by the *style coupé*.[6] He traced this condition to yet another source, "the plethoric form of cumulation and 'periodic' writing" that dominated the newspapers, the main reading matter of most Englishmen. When a reader is repeatedly bombarded with meaningless periodic constructions,

> [he] gradually learns an art of catching at the leading words, and the cardinal or hinge joints of transition, which proclaim the general course of a writer's speculation. Now, it is very true, and is sure to be objected, that, where so much is certain to prove mere iteration and teasing *surplusage*, little can be lost by this or any other process of abridgment. Certainly, as regards the particular subject concerned, there may be no

---

Coleridge's objection to the French/Senecan style had a long tradition behind it. His favorite metaphor for this style, that it was "purposely invented for persons troubled with the asthma," is to be found in Francois de La Mothe Le Vayer's *Considérations sur l'éloquence francoise de ce temps* (1638), written in condemnation of *style coupé* (see Aldo Scaglione, *The Classical Theory of Composition* [Chapel Hill: University of North Carolina Press, 1972], pp. 188–89). For Coleridge, the contrasting and infinitely superior style was represented by the great sixteenth- and seventeenth-century models, Hooker, Bacon, Milton, and Jeremy Taylor: "The unity in these writers is produced by the unity of the subject, and the perpetual growth and evolution of the thoughts, one generating, and explaining, and justifying, the place of another, not, as it is in Seneca, where the thoughts, striking as they are, are merely strung together like beads, without any causation or progression" (*Coleridge's Miscellaneous Criticism*, p. 217). Jerome Christensen has recently written most perceptively on Coleridge's stylistic preferences in prose; see *Coleridge's Blessed Machine of Language* (Ithaca: Cornell University Press, 1981), pp. 205–20.

5. *The Friend*, ii, 152. See also *Letters of Coleridge*, vol. 3, 253–54.

Speaking of the seventeenth-century prose writers Bacon, Milton, Browne, Taylor, and others, William Godwin declared: "Those were the times when authors thought. Every line is pregnant with sense, and the reader is inevitably put to the expense of thinking likewise." Letter to Shelley of 10 December 1812. *The Letters of Percy Bysshe Shelley*, ed. Frederick L. Jones, vol. 1, 341n.

6. "Style" (1840–41), in *Selected Essays on Rhetoric by Thomas De Quincey*, ed. Frederick Burwick, p. 167.

room to apprehend a serious injury. Not there, not in any direct interest, but in a far larger interest . . . the reader suffers a permanent debilitation. . . . [I]t is by reaction upon a man's faculties, it is by the effects reflected upon his judging and reasoning powers, that loose habits of reading tell eventually.[7]

Hazlitt espoused "familiar style" and particularity of diction in opposition to the influence of Johnson, whose prose was still so widely imitated that "we cannot see a lottery puff or a quack advertisement pasted against a wall, that is not perfectly Johnsonian in style."[8] With its "philosophic" diction and its persistently balanced and antithetical structure often unrelated to any genuine balance or antithesis in thought, such prose destroys all discrimination of meaning and of precise connotations: "the words are not fitted to the things, but the things to the words."[9] Such stylistic practices not only fail in significant communication with the reader but pervert the author as well:

Where there is no room for variety, no discrimination, no nicety to be shown in matching the idea with its proper word, there can be no room for taste or elegance. A man must easily learn the art of writing, where every sentence is to be cast in the same mould: where he is only allowed the use of one word he cannot choose wrong, nor will he be in much danger of making himself ridiculous by affectation or false glitter, when, whatever subject he treats of, he must treat it in the same way. This is indeed to wear golden chains for the sake of ornament.[10]

Each of these writers sought to counter the prevailing conditions of prose through dramatic changes in style and ex-

7. *Rhetoric by De Quincey*, p. 162.
8. *Complete Works of William Hazlitt*, ed. P. P. Howe, vol. 5, 105.
9. In contrast, the "words [of Burke] are the most like things" (*Works of Hazlitt*, vol. 7, 309–10). Cf. Wordsworth's objections to Macpherson's natural descriptions where "words are substituted for things" (*Prose Works of William Wordsworth*, ed. W. J. B. Owen and Jane Worthington Smyser, vol. 3, 77); and Coleridge's letter to Godwin of 22 September 1800 (*Letters of Coleridge*, vol. 1, 625–26).
10. *Works of Hazlitt*, vol. 7, 310–11.

pression, of which the adoption of seventeenth-century modes of sentence-structure, particularity and concreteness in word-choice, and "constitutive" rather than merely "decorative" metaphors and images are the most easily documented and widely recognized. However, all these specific devices must be seen as supporting a radical remedial purpose: *to alter profoundly the reader's relation to the prose text.*

Whatever the specific subject matter might happen to be — politics, literary criticism, religion — whatever the form of the individual discourse — familiar essay or extended analytic trea-tise — a main goal of Romantic prose in its most original mani-festations was to oppose the essentially passive activity that prose reading (and writing) had become. The prose writer sought to engage the reader as an active participant, often as the protagonist, in the expository or argumentative process. As we shall see, the reader's heightened awareness of the act of reading is the true subject of a number of Lamb's most impor-tant Elia essays. Coleridge's mature endeavors in prose de-pended on inducing his readers "to retire *into themselves* and make their own minds the objects of their stedfast attention."[11] Wordsworth's "Preface to *Lyrical Ballads*," "Essays upon Epi-taphs," and *Convention of Cintra* required a "participating [of] the truths" or of the historical facts being developed.[12] By ma-nipulations of style and a persistently paradoxical method of ar-gument, Hazlitt left the reader unbalanced and unsettled in his ordinary "logical" response to a topic and thus prepared for fresh confrontation.

If all this seems reminiscent of Wordsworth's well-known attempts to alter the "associations" with which readers ap-proached "original poetry" and to bring those readers to the "exertion of a co-operating *power*" with the poet's,[13] the coinci-dence is not accidental. Romantic literary opinion did not draw particularly sharp lines of differentiation between "poetry" and

11. *The Friend*, ii, 151.
12. *Prose Works of Wordsworth*, vol. 2, 68.
13. Ibid., vol. 3, 81–82.

the "impassioned, eloquent, and powerful" prose for which Wordsworth yearned in 1816. The heroes of romantic prose, sixteenth and seventeenth-century writers from Hooker to Jeremy Taylor and in more recent times Edmund Burke, were "almost poets."

Although there is no body of romantic theorizing about prose to rival the extensive and brilliantly original exposition of poetic theory, early nineteenth-century speculation on prose does have its own integrity. It is significant that most speculation is found in the discussion of poetry, specifically in attempts to delineate the differences between "poetic" and other forms of discourse. The most obvious and superficial difference, the presence or absence of rhyme or meter, is not seen as the distinguishing factor. On the one hand, Coleridge argued that "poetry of the highest kind may exist without metre;" on the other hand, Wordsworth declared that "lines and passages of metre so naturally occur in writing prose, that it would be scarcely possible to avoid them, even were it desirable."[14] For Hazlitt,

> All is not poetry that passes for such: nor does verse make the whole difference between poetry and prose. The Iliad does not cease to be poetry in a literal translation; and Addison's Campaign has been very properly denominated a Gazette in rhyme.[15]

Shelley boldly declared that "the popular division into prose and verse, is inadmissible in accurate philosophy," and he went on to include Bacon and Plato among poets on the basis of an "harmonious recurrence of sound" in their writings.[16]

14. *Biographia Literaria*, ed. James Engell and W. Jackson Bate, *Works of Coleridge*, vol. 7, ii, 14; *Prose Works of Wordsworth*, vol. 1, 135. Behind the Wordsworth passage immediately lies William Enfield's essay "Is Verse Essential to Poetry?" in the *Monthly Magazine* 2 (1796), 453–56.

15. *Works of Hazlitt*, vol. 5, 13.

16. Fanny Delisle, *A Study of Shelley's A Defence of Poetry: A Textual and Critical Evaluation*, vol. 1, 57–62. Similar remarks in Sidney's *Defence of Poetry* have been long cited as a source for Shelley; Delisle adds Lord Monboddo's *On the Origin and Progress of Language* (1773–92).

Somewhat more to the point was the traditionally defined difference in purposes or ends. It was commonly perceived that "the immediate purpose" of poetry was to please, of prose to instruct or to convince; the one seeks beauty, the other truth.[17] Yet even this is not quite accurate, as Coleridge argued in *Biographia Literaria*:

> The writings of PLATO, and Bishop TAYLOR, and the "Theoria Sacra" of BURNET, furnish undeniable proofs that poetry of the highest kind may exist . . . without the contradistinguishing objects of a poem. The first chapter of Isaiah (indeed a very large portion of the whole book) is poetry in the most emphatic sense; yet it would be not less irrational than strange to assert, that pleasure, and not truth, was the immediate object of the prophet.[18]

The ultimate refinement involved two distinctions. First, "poetry" was clearly to be distinguished not from nonmetrical language or from instructive discourse but from a very specifically limited application of such language or discourse: "science," "philosophy," and "matter of fact."[19] The difference here lay in the writer's attitude toward both his subject matter and his reader. In all "argumentative and consecutive works," to use Coleridge's phrase,[20] the writer is concerned only with the logical consistency of his propositions or the order of his expository material; he addresses himself solely to the "understanding" or the logical faculty of his reader, vigorously excluding all passionate and imaginative appeals through the heightenings of affective diction or images. In contrast, in "eloquent prose-poetry," the

17. *Biographia Literaria*, ii, 12–13; *Notebooks of Coleridge*, entries 4111–12 (October-November 1811); *Works of Hazlitt*, vol. 5, 15n; vol. 12, 8–11.

18. *Biographia Literaria*, ii, 14–15.

19. Enfield, "Is Verse Essential," 456; *Prose Works of Wordsworth*, vol. 1, 135n; *Works of Hazlitt*, vol. 5, 13. The distinction has also been located in Condillac's *De l'art d'ecrire* (1775); see Hans Aarsleff, "Wordsworth, Language, and Romanticism," 221–23.

20. *Biographia Literaria*, ii, 60.

writer has a passionate apprehension of the thing or the idea he wishes to communicate, and this apprehension is reflected in the highly imaginative language he employs or in a sentence structure that contagiously reveals the drama of the evolving thought for the deeper-than-logical engagement of the reader.

The second distinction, most memorably developed by Coleridge, was between "poetry" and a "poem." The very presence of meter in a poem requires a more "studied selection and artificial arrangement" of all the elements of the work (sentence-structure, syntax, choice and arrangement of words, for example) to excite "a more continuous and equal attention, than the language of prose aims at, whether colloquial or written."[21]

For the romantics, Edmund Burke was the supreme example of "eloquent prose-poetry" in their own lifetime. Burke was the practitioner of a mode of discourse whose purpose certainly was conviction rather than beauty, but which in its imaginative components "went the nearest to the verge of poetry."[22] As early as 1796 Coleridge had praised Burke for the affective and imaginative components in his argumentation: "he has secured the aids of sympathy to his cause by the warmth of his own emotions, and delighted the imagination of his readers by a multitude and rapid succession of remote analogies. It seems characteristic of true eloquence, to reason *in* metaphors."[23] In 1798, as Hazlitt recalls, Coleridge declared Burke to be "almost a poet."[24] Hazlitt himself wrote extensively on Burke's prose, which for him was "most perfect":

> He works the most striking effects out of the most unpromising materials, by the mere activity of his mind. He rises with the lofty, descends with the mean, luxuriates in beauty, gloats over deformity. It is all the same to him, so that he loses no

21. Ibid., 15.
22. *Works of Hazlitt*, vol. 12, 10.
23. *The Watchman*, ed. Lewis Patton, *Works of Samuel Taylor Coleridge*, vol. 2, 30–31.
24. *Works of Hazlitt*, vol. 17, 111.

particle of the exact, characteristic, extreme impression of the thing he writes about, and that he communicates this to the reader, after exhausting every possible mode of illustration, plain or abstracted, figurative or literal.[25]

Jeremy Taylor was another admired model of "eloquent prose-poetry," the imaginative richness of his images and metaphors almost, as in the case of Burke, muting the purpose of conviction that directed his works. In 1809, Coleridge described Taylor as "the most eloquent of our Writers (I had almost said of our Poets)."[26] The overlapping of poetry and prose in romantic literary opinion is perhaps nowhere clearer than in Hazlitt's comment about Taylor and some other of "the old divines": these "old English prose-writers (who were not poets) are the best, and, at the same time, the most *poetical* in the favourable sense."[27]

This overlapping and blurring of the lines of distinction between poetry and prose meant for the romantic prose writer, just as for the romantic poet, the self-imposed goal of addressing the reader and of involving him with the linguistic materials on several levels: "the excellence of writing," Wordsworth declared in 1810, "*whether in prose or verse*, consists in a conjunction of Reason and Passion."[28] If the prose writer did not bring "the whole soul of man into activity," as did Coleridge's "ideal" poet, he certainly sought to appeal to more than one faculty of the reader. If prose could not command of its reader the same level of "continuous and equal attention" that a poem could, it is clear that the romantic prose writer was asking for a degree of "attention" and involvement in the prose process that was radi-

---

25. Ibid., vol. 12, 10. This is from an essay of the 1820s; for a similar acknowledgment of Burke's imaginative capacity dating from 1807, see vol. 7, 309–10.

26. *The Friend*, ii, 176n. See also *The Letters of Charles and Mary Anne Lamb*, ed. Edwin W. Marrs, Jr., vol. 2, 4–6, 35–36.

27. *Works of Hazlitt*, vol. 12, 17.

28. *Prose Works of Wordsworth*, vol. 2, 85. My italics.

cally at odds with the desultory habits of the contemporary reader. Much of the most original prose of the early nineteenth century undertook the education of the reader *as reader* by attempting to break conventional habits of response, in some cases by engineering a direct confrontation with those habits. Lamb's Elia essays are a dramatic instance of this confrontation.

2. ELIA AND THE TRANSFORMED READER

READER, in thy passage from the Bank — where thou hast been receiving thy half-yearly dividends (supposing thou art a lean annuitant like myself) — to the Flower Pot, to secure a place for Dalston, or Shacklewell, or some other thy suburban retreat northerly, — didst thou never observe a melancholy looking, handsome, brick and stone edifice, to the left — where Threadneedle-street abuts upon Bishopsgate? I dare say thou hast often admired its magnificent portals ever gaping wide, and disclosing to view a grave court, with cloisters, and pillars, with few or no traces of goers-in or comers-out — a desolation something like Balclutha's.°
° I passed by the walls of Balclutha, and they were desolate —
OSSIAN.

The first sentence of this first paragraph of the first Elia essay, "The South-Sea House" (August 1820),[1] testifies to Lamb's central preoccupation with his reader; it also indicates the strenuous imaginative and rhetorical activity in which the reader unexpectedly finds himself involved. Here the reader is not only addressed with the first word but immediately cast into a particular role, a "lean annuitant like myself." Thus Elia and reader are initially drawn together in an identity derived from a *monetary* tie to the past. The reader is made to assume still fur-

1. All quotations from the Elia essays are from the revised versions in the collections: *Elia: Essays Which Have Appeared Under That Signature in the London Magazine* (1823) and *The Last Essays of Elia* (1833), as reproduced in the second volume of *The Works of Charles and Mary Lamb*, ed. E. V. Lucas, 7 vols. (London: Methuen and Company 1903–1905). In the case of "The South-Sea House," "Oxford in the Vacation," and "Blakesmoor in H——shire," the variations between the original *London Magazine* versions and the texts of 1823 and 1833 are not significant for the purposes of my exposition.

ther definition in this opening sentence: his concern with his surroundings is, like his tie to the past, purely utilitarian; he visits the "Bank" for his money, moves to the "Flower Pot" for his coach, then heads for his home.

What Elia has done is arrest the reader on this carefully ordered journey and abruptly turn his eye out of its ordinary path to "observe" a building. This building is first described as it would initially occur to our utilitarian reader, simply as a physical object, "a brick-and-stone edifice" having meaning in relation to other more familiar things: "to the left — where Threadneedle street abuts upon Bishopsgate." The adjectives "melancholy looking, handsome" are the only suggestion thus far of any response to the building other than as physical object awkwardly glimpsed in an arrested journey. However, in the second sentence, the reader's reaction is switched from relatively passive and uncertain "observation" ("didst you never observe") to assumed "admiration" ("I dare say thou hast often admired"), with a corresponding change in the descriptive language: from "handsome" to "magnificent," and from "melancholy" to the grandeur of mythic "desolation."

This switch in response and language is simultaneous with a switch in physical perspective. In the first sentence, the reader saw the building only in relation to other exterior things; in the second, the eye travels through "magnificent portals" to "a grave court, with cloisters, and pillars" to note the parts of the building in relation to each other. An internal, integral view is substituted for an external comparative glimpse. This transformation of response reaches its climax with the final words of the paragraph, "a desolation something like Balclutha's." The language of normative, utilitarian discourse that has prevailed thus far — of "half-yearly dividends," "suburban retreats," "brick and stone edifice," Threadneedle-street, and Bishopsgate — proves insufficient to capture the effect of the building. Such language must be supplanted now by resonant imaginative allusion.

The conclusion of this paragraph, as are the conclusions of

all of Lamb's rhetorically more strenuous paragraphs involving reader-transformation, is rich in tone and in reference. The allusion to Balclutha is apposite in several ways: Lamb's footnote prevents us from missing the source as Ossian, thus establishing a purely *imaginative* tie to a more distant past than the source of the capital of our "lean annuitant"; at the same time, the footnote also prevents us from forgetting that this allusion is to Macpherson's famous hoax, thus introducing a note of the anticlimactic and mock-heroic into the climactic reference. The entire essay, as we shall see, is punctuated with references to other frauds and hoaxes as well as with frequent passages of ironic and humorous tone. These all serve to ease and to beguile the reader as he is being led to adopt a perspective radically different from the mundane, unimaginative concerns of the first sentence. Such a tactic is already at work in the opening paragraph.

The reader's experience of the first paragraph is reproduced and intensified in the second paragraph:

> This was once a house of trade, — a centre of busy interests. The throng of merchants was here — the quick pulse of gain — and here some forms of business are still kept up, though the soul be long since fled. Here are still to be seen stately porticos; imposing staircases; offices roomy as the state apartments in palaces — deserted, or thinly peopled with a few straggling clerks; the still more sacred interiors of court and committee rooms, with venerable faces of beadles, doorkeepers — directors seated in form on solemn days (to proclaim a dead dividend,) at long worm-eaten tables, that have been mahogany, with tarnished gilt-leather coverings, supporting massy silver inkstands long since dry; — the oaken wainscots hung with pictures of deceased governors and subgovernors, of queen Anne, and the two first monarchs of the Brunswick dynasty; — huge charts, which subsequent discoveries have antiquated; — dusty maps of Mexico, dim as dreams, — and soundings of the Bay of Panama! — The long passages hung with buckets, appended, in idle row, to walls, whose substance might defy any, short of the last, conflagra-

tion: — with vast ranges of cellarage under all, where dollars and pieces of eight once lay, an "unsunned heap," for Mammon to have solaced his solitary heart withal, — long since dissipated, or scattered into air at the blast of the breaking of that famous BUBBLE. — —

The reproduction is evident first in the movement from utilitarian concerns and language at the start of the paragraph — "house of trade," "centre of busy interests," "throng of merchants," "quick pulse of gain" — to evocative images, Biblical allusion, and poetic quotation toward the end. This verbal change both accompanies and embodies a steady physical movement through *interior* "stately porticos" (paralleling the "magnificent portals" of the *outer* facade in the first paragraph) to still "more sacred interiors," and finally into the very cellars where the wealth and hence the source of the life of the House resided.

The second paragraph ends with the first direct reference to the South-Sea Bubble, the famous eighteenth-century *financial* hoax (paralleling the similarly climactic reference of the previous paragraph to that century's most famous *literary* hoax). Here, however, the effect is not to mock the highly evocative experience, the rich inward movement to magnificence, but to remind the reader that the utilitarian basis of that magnificence is gone. For the success of his experience within the essay, the reader must shed completely his unimaginative, spectator-like status. That has quietly begun here. A dramatic further step in the process comes with the opening of the next paragraph.

The third paragraph begins innocently enough with the statement, "such is the SOUTH-SEA HOUSE." The building originally observed so casually now stands rendered and identified before us. But with the second sentence this apparently secure reality with all its details presented to us as tangible is whisked away; we are told that the building exists now only in its mental reconstruction by Elia and reader: "At least, such it was forty years ago, when I knew it, — a magnificent relic!" The building has been entirely internalized and imaginatively "fabricated." Elia can risk this removal of his originally utilitarian reader from the secure world of physical fact because of the strength of the imaginative movement of the two previous paragraphs, along with the attendant humor to ease the passage.

The succeeding sentences of the third paragraph might seem to endanger the position achieved, by their description of the probable further physical retreat of the house from its original splendor or even from its more recent heroic desolation recreated in imagination:

> Time, I take for granted, has not freshened it. No wind has resuscitated the face of the sleeping waters. A thicker crust by this time stagnates upon it. The moths, that were then battening upon its obsolete ledgers and day-books, have rested from their depredations, but other light generations have succeeded, making fine fretwork among their single and double entries. Layers of dust have accumulated (a superfoetation of dirt!) upon the old layers.

But again Elia is willing to risk this and even to use a more openly humorous tone because the arrest of his reader from present utilitarian concerns is now sufficiently secure. In fact, with the final lines of this paragraph, any attempt to know the exact details of the Bubble, something that might well have previously constituted the only interest for the reader in the South-Sea House, is seen as an activity bordering on sacrilege ("some curious finger . . . with less hallowed curiosity, seeking to unveil some of the mysteries of that tremendous HOAX"). Instead, the only response to the Bubble can be "incredulous admiration."

The brevity of the fourth paragraph after the elaborateness of the preceding three paragraphs is a sign of its summary function: "Peace to the manes of the BUBBLE! Silence and destitution are upon thy walls, proud house, for a memorial!" Even in its mock-heroic tone, the first apostrophe signals the end to any further consideration of the house in its primary historic significance and reality. It exists hereafter, not for historic investigation but for imaginative possession in its later fragmented state.

In short, the house has become one pole in a psychological drama between worldly concerns and imaginative exercise; the strength of its imaginative reality is found in the direct address to the house in the second apostrophe.

A striking indication of the distance we have traveled from the start is provided by the opening of the fifth paragraph. In the first paragraph the reader had virtually ignored the house in his excursion from the more relevant "Bank" to the "Flower Pot," or he saw it only in relation to the stronger present realities of Threadneedle-street and Bishopsgate. Now, however, those present realities, and in fact the entire mercantile world, are seen — and judged — from the perspective of the house:

> Situated as thou art, in the very heart of stirring and living commerce, — amid the fret and fever of speculation — with the Bank, and the 'Change, and the India-house about thee, in the hey-day of present prosperity, with their important faces, as it were, insulting thee, their *poor neighbour out of business* — to the idle and merely contemplative, — to such as me, old house! there is a charm in thy quiet: — a cessation — a coolness from business — an indolence almost cloistral — which is delightful!

The absence of the house from the world of commerce, which initially had made it an almost disregarded object, now serves to reveal the competitive "fret and fever" of that very world and its proud presumption that its utilitarian values are paramount. Those values are dismissed in this passage for the "charm and delight" provided by the house. As the paragraph continues, Elia carries the reader far beyond "charm and delight" to the moral and religious values incarnated in this temple of memory:

> With what reverence have I paced thy great bare rooms and courts at eventide! They spoke of the past. . . . [T]hy great dead tomes, which scarce three degenerate clerks of the present day could lift from their enshrining shelves . . . with pious sentences at the beginning, without which our religious ancestors never ventured to open a book of business, or bill of lading . . . are very agreeable and edifying spectacles.

This dramatic movement to the greater positive value of the house for its evocation of a morally heightened life is, to be sure, accompanied by the mock-heroic, humorous tone we have noted before in crucial passages of mental and imaginative advance. It is found here especially in the concluding sentences of the paragraph:

> I can look upon these defunct dragons with complacency. Thy heavy odd-shaped ivory-handled pen-knives (our ancestors had every thing on a larger scale than we have hearts for) are as good as any thing from Herculaneum. The pounce-boxes of our days have gone retrograde.

Eventually, however, as the imaginative values of the house are more thoroughly absorbed, the mock-heroic tone disappears or is recalled only to be immediately dispatched. The agents for this final achievement are the former inhabitants of the house, who enact (as exempla for the reader) complete transformation of *their* limited existences by the strength of *their* imaginative recreation of the past, a past that exists — it should be noted — only within; just as the reality of the house for the reader exists only in his imaginative reconstruction of it from the skillful arrangement of black-and-white marks on the page.

In keeping with the consistent pattern of the essay, the clerks of the South-Sea House are initially seen from the "outside" perspective of their difference from those in offices of more recent times. They are accordingly presented as eccentric and inconsequential:

> They were mostly (for the establishment did not admit of superfluous salaries) bachelors. Generally (for they had not much to do) persons of a curious and speculative turn of mind. Humorists, for they were of all descriptions; and, not having been brought together in early life (which has a tendency to assimilate the members of corporate bodies to each other), but, for the most part, placed in this house in ripe or middle age, they necessarily carried into it their separate habits and oddities, unqualified, if I may so speak, as into a com-

mon stock. Hence they formed a sort of Noah's ark. Odd
fishes. A lay-monastery. Domestic retainers in a great house,
kept more for show than use. Yet pleasant fellows, full of
chat — and not a few among them had arrived at considerable
proficiency on the German flute.

The three major exempla — Evans the cashier, Tame his deputy,
and John Tipp the accountant — are subjected to similar descriptive processes. First, their odd external appearance or behavior is noted, then the mental preoccupations are examined
that more truly establish their identities for themselves, for Elia,
and eventually for the transformed reader.

Evans is introduced in all his ludicrously antiquated appearance and "neurotic" behavior:

> He wore his hair, to the last, powdered and frizzed out, in
> the fashion which I remember to have seen in caricatures of
> what were termed, in my young days, *Maccaronies*. He was
> the last of that race of beaux. Melancholy as a gib-cat over
> his counter all the forenoon, I think I see him, making up his
> cash (as they call it) with tremulous fingers, as if he feared
> every one about him was a defaulter; in his hypochondry
> ready to imagine himself one; haunted, at least, with the idea
> of the possibility of his becoming one.

As the paragraph continues, we learn that Evans is the subject
of something other than ridicule in his after-office role as "eloquent" describer of the past:

> How would he dilate into secret history! His countryman,
> Pennant himself, in particular, could not be more eloquent
> than he in relation to old and new London — the site of
> old theatres, churches, streets gone to decay — where Rosa-
> mond's pond stood — the Mulberry-gardens — and the Con-
> duit in Cheap — with many a pleasant anecdote, derived from
> paternal tradition, of those grotesque figures which Hogarth
> has immortalized in his picture of *Noon*, — the worthy descen-
> dants of those heroic confessors, who, flying to this country,
> from the wrath of Louis the Fourteenth and his dragoons,

> kept alive the flame of pure religion in the sheltering obscurities of Hog-lane, and the vicinity of the Seven Dials!

The final detail is a complex example of imaginative and artistic re-creation, in some sense a model of the procedure of the entire essay. First, Evans preserves and passes on "paternal tradition" that can see "heroic confessors" buried beneath "grotesque figures." Then, correspondingly, the "heroic confessors" preserve the "flame of pure religion in the sheltering obscurities of Hog-lane." Elia himself as artist preserves and "immortalizes" the grotesque Evans, just as the artist Hogarth "immortalized" the "grotesque" descendants. And Elia teaches us how to "read" Evans, as Evans taught his listeners how to "read" Hogarth; that is, how to find the "secret" of the history of the figures there represented. For Elia, Evans, and Hogarth, that "secret" was a religious and imaginative dedication to values from the past transcending present limited surroundings.

The second of the clerks, Thomas Tame, similarly reveals a split between a redeeming internal strength derived from dedication to the past and current severe limitations. Although he treats others with condescension,

> his intellect was of the shallowest order. It did not reach to a saw or a proverb. His mind was in its original state of white paper. A sucking babe might have posed him. What was it then [that accounted for his condescension]? Was he rich? Alas, no! Thomas Tame was very poor.

Both Tame and his wife assume an air of self-respect and dignified deportment through their dedication to her descent from the noble family of the Radcliffes, who, like the Huguenots of the previous paragraph, were "illustrious but unfortunate" in suffering for religious conviction. (In this case, James Radcliffe, the last Earl of Derwentwater, was executed for his support of the Catholic Pretender.) Just as the Huguenots "kept alive the flame of pure religion in the sheltering *obscurities* of Hog-lane," so, too, the memory of his noble ancestors was kept alive by Thomas Tame, cheering him "in the night of intellect, and in the *obscurity* of [his] station!"[2] In one sense, of course, the noble deportment of the simple-minded Tame is a fraud, like the Ossianic poems and the South-Sea House itself. But in another sense, it is a redeeming source of strength and protection against his actual irrelevance:

> This [secret] was to you instead of riches, instead of rank, instead of glittering attainments: and it was worth them altogether. You insulted none with it; but, while you wore it as a piece of defensive armour only, no insult likewise could reach you through it.

The value of this strength can be captured by Elia, in the last words on the Tames, only by evoking once again the language of heroic imaginative literature: *Decus et solamen.*[3]

The accountant John Tipp lacked the noble blood of Tame and the historical imagination of Evans. Still, he achieved an identity by the "intensity" of his dedication to his "role" as accountant, despite his clear awareness of the irrelevance of the financial operations in the decayed establishment. Although he lacked courage ("Nature certainly had been pleased to endow John Tipp with a sufficient measure of the principle of self-preservation"), the "unerring heart" that lay beneath the "intensity" of his embrace of his role meant that "for lucre, or for intimidation, he [never] forsook friend or principle." Again, Elia reveals to us the rich human quality beneath the ludicrous or the banal; and again, it is a quality derived from the imaginative possession of a past importance.

In summary, Elia describes Evans, Tame, and Tipp, as well as five others he treats more briefly, as figures "from the dusty dead, in whom common qualities become uncommon." The statement is significant; when seen from the perspective of the imaginative re-creation of the past that has been evolved by the essay and demonstrated by each of the characters, the ordinary becomes extraordinary. So far from the imaginative

2. My italics.
3. *Aeneid*, 10, 858–59.

reconstruction being purely fanciful, the activity of the essay leads to a discovery of truth, a freshness of perception about human experience.

With this position now secured, Lamb can at the close of the essay test his reader's achievement by raising the suggestion that the entire procedure has been a fraud, a "solemn mockery," a "[fooling of] the reader to the top of his bent" (echoing a remark about Rosencrantz, Guildenstern, and Polonius made by Hamlet,[4] who was no more deceived by those conspirators than is the reader by Elia at this point). He even suggests that there has been no reality to these characters at all: "Reader, what if I had been playing with thee all this while — peradventure the very *names*, which I have summoned up before thee, are fantastic — insubstantial." The answer Elia provides in the final paragraph is one the reader is now more than willing to second: "Be satisfied that something answering to them has had a being. Their importance is from the past." Whether the representation of these particular characters is in all respects true or not, the stimulation of our imaginative capacity through aesthetic material provokes us to recognize and to affirm the worth and the dignity of the individual life, no matter how banal or eccentric it may seem. The reading of the essay is the exercise of our often buried instinct for that worth and dignity.

* * *

"Oxford in the Vacation" (October 1820), the second of the Elia essays, is an even more radical example of Lamb's attempted redirection and transformation of the reader.[5] The essay is specifically about habits of reading and of responding to imaginatively charged material. In effect, "Oxford" completes the training of the reader begun in "the South-Sea House" and

4. *Hamlet*, act 3, sc. 2, line 401.
5. Gerald Monsman has explored a quite different thematic relationship and connection between "The South-Sea House" and "Oxford in the Vacation"; see *Confessions of a Prosaic Dreamer: Charles Lamb's Art of Autobiography*, pp. 37–54. Some of Monsman's remarks on "Oxford" were anticipated by my essay "Drama and Rhetoric in Lamb's Essays of the Imagination," 696–702.

prepares him for the long series of Elia essays to follow, in which, with one or two exceptions,[6] the reader himself will not again be the central subject of concern. His training having been accomplished in the critically programmatic first two essays, he is now presumably equipped to respond properly to the personality and to the experience of the apparently eccentric and inconsequential Elia himself — to his "imperfect sympathies," his fondness for old china or Mrs. Battle, and his reactions to his retirement, to new year's eve, and to witches and other night fears.

> CASTING a preparatory glance at the bottom of this article — as the wary connoisseur in prints, with cursory eye (which, while it reads, seems as though it read not,) never fails to consult the *quis sculpsit* in the corner, before he pronounces some rare piece to be a Vivares, or a Woollet — methinks I hear you exclaim, Reader, *Who is Elia?*

In the initial paragraph of this second Elia essay, the reader is not required to assume, as in "South-Sea House," an artificial and fanciful identity; he is simply confronted with himself in the very act of reading the text before him. To be sure, his habits of reading are delineated, reflecting the worldly bias of the observer of the South-Sea House. As the simile of the connoisseur suggests, the reader (a "you" at this point separate from Elia the "I") is primarily interested in the external identity and reputation of the artist, not in the imaginative values of the product before him. (If we take the simile in its full implications, the reader is at quite a distance from the "reality" of the work of art; for the connoisseur is interested only in the engraver, not in the original artist, much less in the imaginative subject itself.) The reader wishes to judge the work of art in worldly terms before experiencing it, or possibly in place of experiencing it. The italicized exclamatory question "*Who is*

---

6. "On the Artificial Comedy of the Last Century" (April 1822) is a notable example. See "Drama and Rhetoric in Lamb's Essays of the Imagination," pp. 687–96.

Elia?" indicates the irritation of the reader that the precise worldly identity here for once eludes him.

Confounded by the text before him, the reader draws on the suggestion of the preceding essay and triumphantly reduces Elia to his mundane identity:

> Because in my last I tried to divert thee with some half-forgotten humours of some old clerks defunct, in an old house of business, long since gone to decay, doubtless you have already set me down in your mind as one of the self-same college — a votary of the desk — a notched and cropt scrivener — one that sucks his sustenance, as certain sick persons are said to do, through a quill.

With the third paragraph, a shift in perspective occurs away from the "you" to Elia the "I," who initially accepts the radical movement and the success of the reader in submerging the artist's identity in external fact: "Well, I do agnize something of the sort," Elia declares. "I confess," begins the second sentence and seems to confirm the submission; but, as the sentence continues, we learn that Elia's employment as a clerk is simply "my humour, my fancy." His true identity and profession are found in his work as artist:

> I confess that it is my humour, my fancy — in the forepart of the day, when the mind of your man of letters requires some relaxation — (and none better than such as at first sight seems most abhorrent from his beloved studies) — to while away some good hours of my time in the contemplation of indigos, cottons, raw silks, piece-goods, flowered or otherwise.

Thus, instead of economic reality submerging his artistic identity, that identity flies free of reality, which functions largely to further the flight. By the end of the paragraph Elia has triumphantly escaped from the role in which the reader would have liked to place him. However, the playful tone of the paragraph must be carefully observed, most notably in the asterisks that fill out the ways in which Elia's employment supports his literary activity, as well as the lighthearted language describing his writing:

> In the first place ° ° ° ° and then it sends you home with such increased appetite to your books ° ° ° ° not to say, that your outside sheets, and waste wrappers of foolscap, do receive into them, most kindly and naturally, the impression of sonnets, epigrams, *essays* — so that the very parings of the counting-house are, in some sort, the settings up of an author. The enfranchised quill, that has plodded all the morning among the cart-rucks of figures and cyphers, frisks and curvets so at its ease over the flowery carpet-ground of a midnight dissertation. — It feels its promotion. ° ° ° ° So that you see, upon the whole, the literary dignity of *Elia* is very little, if at all, compromised in the condescension.

The same playfulness is found in the succeeding two paragraphs, in which we move still further away from the restrictions of present external reality into a freer, holier, and more imaginatively charged world of the past and of childhood. Specifically, Elia is recalling his days at Christ's Hospital. Like his present world of business, it was a place of limits and restriction; but it contained "consolatory interstices, and sprinklings of freedom" in the form of holy-days. Elia is simultaneously recovering those reverent breaks of freedom and smiling at the child's very response to them:

> There was Paul, and Stephen, and Barnabas . . . we were used to keep all their days holy, as long back as I was at school at Christ's. I remember their effigies, by the same token, in the old *Basket* Prayer Book. There hung Peter in his uneasy posture — holy Bartlemy in the troublesome act of flaying, after the famous Marsyas by Spagnoletti. — I honoured them all, and could almost have wept the defalcation of Iscariot — so much did we love to keep holy memories sacred: — only methought I a little grudged at the coalition of the *better Jude* with Simon — clubbing (as it were) their sanctities together, to make up one poor gaudy-day between them — as an economy unworthy of the dispensation.

Just as at the beginning of "The South-Sea House," humor functions here as a way of making more acceptable to the "wary" reader the very movement away from his limited response. It is a way of preparing the "you" (who is soon to become a "we" with Elia) for Oxford, where the complete loss of our time-bound worldly identity becomes possible. By the end of the fifth paragraph, Elia has indeed arrived at "the heart of learning, under the shadow of the mighty Bodley." Significantly, it is the library at which Elia first arrives and which remains a central focus hereafter in the essay; for it is through reading that our ordinary limited perspective on life can be displaced. That experience is illustrated in the very act of reading this essay, as the next two paragraphs demonstrate.

These paragraphs, which re-create Elia's initial experience at Oxford, are progressive in their development. The first is dominated by "I" and recounts still playfully the transformation of Elia from humble student to Seraphic Doctor. At one point the reader participates in the play, joining both Oxford students and Elia, who are all on vacation: "Their vacation, too, at this time of the year, falls in so pat with *ours*." The same generalizing of Elia's experience becomes more consistent in the next paragraph:

> The walks at these times are so much one's own — the tall trees of Christ's, the groves of Magdalen! The halls deserted, and with open doors, inviting one to slip in unperceived, and pay a devoir to some Founder, or noble or royal Benefactress (that should have been ours) whose portrait seems to smile upon their overlooked beadsman, and to adopt me for their own.

The reader has moved more fully into Elia's experience, an internal, imaginative movement paralleling the external, physical movement from the outside walks and groves into the halls of the colleges and, finally, into the innermost recesses of the kitchens. (One recalls a similar movement in the early stages of the reader's experience with the South-Sea House.) The movement is also further into the past, "four centuries ago" to the time of Chaucer, by whose imagination Elia is now controlled: "Not the meanest minister among the dishes but is hallowed to me through his imagination, and the Cook goes forth a Manciple." This strategy of one imaginative agent supplanting another, recalling the roles of Evans, Tame, and Tipp in the previous essay, is repeated later in the essay with another "grotesque" figure, George Dyer, an inhabitant of Oxford.

In paragraphs eight and nine, the onward movement of the essay ceases for the moment as Elia questions the pattern that has been evolving.

> Antiquity! thou wondrous charm, what are thou? that, being nothing, art every thing! When thou *wert*, thou wert not antiquity — then thou wert nothing, but hadst a remoter *antiquity*, as thou called'st it, to look back to with blind veneration; thou thyself being to thyself flat, jejune, *modern*! What mystery lurks in this retroversion? or what half Januses are we, that cannot look forward with the same idolatry with which we for ever revert!

This questioning of the imaginative participation in antiquity through literature as an escape from "our" limited time-bound identities acts not to destroy the movement but to strengthen it, to unite "us" still more to the past; for this "retroversion" is seen as the operation of a universal and timeless psychological process. In short, the activity in which Elia and the reader have been engaged, in part at least fancifully, is now rooted in psychological fact; links of a more permanent and internal sort have been made between us and the world we seek to evoke. And that world is, after all, the world of common humanity, as paragraph nine declares:

> What were thy *dark ages*? Surely the sun rose as brightly then as now, and man got him to his work in the morning. Why is it we can never hear mention of them without an accompanying feeling, as though a palpable obscure had dimmed the face of things, and that our ancestors wandered to and fro groping!

In the "The South-Sea House," "common qualities became uncommon"; here the foreign becomes familiar. Both have a similar source: because of the movement of "our" minds away from external utilitarian standards, reality is stripped of its banality; the strange, as well as the familiar, becomes humanly relevant and fresh. In each case, our understanding and responsiveness to human experience in general is immeasurably advanced.

With this weight of psychological probability now supporting him, Elia resumes the onward movement and with it the final step in preparation for the entrance of George Dyer, the purest embodiment of an identity at odds with external limiting reality. We are once again in the library. With the same operation of humor he had used before at such crucial moments of transition, Elia describes the library as a "middle state," where the souls of the writers rest between their earthly existence and their ultimate remove in death, much like the "middle state," between the claims of external reality and a sympathetic embrace of all human experience, that Elia and the reader have now reached. It is a paradisaic state, which might be destroyed, as Elia tells us, by bringing to bear on it the demands of our limited reality:

> I do not want to handle, to profane the leaves, their winding-sheets. I could as soon dislodge a shade. I seem to inhale learning, walking amid their foliage; and the odour of their old moth-scented coverings is fragrant as the first bloom of those sciential apples which grew amid the happy orchard.

With "G.D.," who now enters the essay, there is no danger of destroying the vision, for his is a total commitment. Like our initial view of the inhabitants of the South-Sea House, "G.D." is first seen as grotesque and humorous; he is viewed as "absent" from "our" world, rather than inhabiting a world of paramount value of his own: "I found [him] busy as a moth," Elia tells us,

> over some rotten archive, rummaged out of some seldom-explored press, in a nook at Oriel. With long poring, he is

grown almost into a book. He stood as passive as one by the side of the old shelves. I longed to new-coat him in Russia, and assign him his place. He might have mustered for a tall Scapula.

Succeeding paragraphs establish further George Dyer's ludicrous absence from reality. However, in the final two paragraphs of the essay, "G.D.'s" world triumphantly asserts itself.

As the opening of paragraph sixteen makes clear, it is not now a matter of "absence" from, but of "presence" in: "For with G.D. — to be absent from the body, is sometimes (not to speak it profanely) to be present with the Lord." The world of the Lord that "G.D." inhabits is first unfolded while we are still in our world observing him: "At the very time when, personally encountering thee, he passes on with no recognition — or, being stopped, starts like a thing surprised — at that moment, reader . . ."; with that moment, the world of "G.D." fully emerges, and "we" are there in his generous thoughts:

> at that moment, reader, he is . . . devising some plan of amelioration to thy country, or thy species — peradventure meditating some individual kindness or courtesy, to be done to *thee thyself*, the returning consciousness of which made him to start so guiltily at thy obtruded personal presence.

The final paragraph summarizes and completes the process. It moves from negative ("He cares not much for Bath. He is out of his element at Buxton, Scarborough, or at Harrowgate") to positive ("The Cam and the Isis are to him 'better than all the waters of Damascus'"); and from secular watering places to the Delectable Mountains and the House Beautiful, where "G.D." may point out to us the way to secular salvation, the expansion of one's humanity that the imaginative response to the past through literature provides. It is through the mind of the reader, who originally attempted to draw the artist back into Vanity Fair, that the moral values of "G.D.'s" world are finally expressed: "and when he goes about with *you* to show *you* the halls and colleges, *you* think *you* have with *you* the Interpreter at the House Beautiful."[7]

*   *   *

Although it was not the first written of the works included in *Last Essays of Elia* (1833) — such distinguished essays as "Old China" and "The Old Margate Hoy" preceded it in point of composition and magazine appearance — "Blakesmoor in H—shire" (September 1824)[8] stood first in the volume. The choice was appropriate and, I would venture, deliberate on Lamb's part. "Blakesmoor" is parallel in subject with the "South-Sea House," the first essay in the 1823 volume: both involve an imaginative encounter with an old building. The experience here, however, is entirely personal to Elia. Proper response to this experience and proper understanding of the drama require the preparation of the reader advanced in the opening essays of the earlier series.

The essay opens with a paragraph clearly revealing the difference in reader-author relationship. In "The South-Sea House" and "Oxford in the Vacation," the reader had to be subtly moved toward Elia's perspective; here there are shared assumptions from the start. Notice the effortlessness of the shift from "I" to "we" to "you," and in the final image the readily transformable nature of the reader under imaginative stimulus:

> I do not know a pleasure more affecting than to range at will over the deserted apartments of some fine old family mansion. The traces of extinct grandeur admit of a better passion than envy: and contemplations on the good and great, whom we fancy in succession to have been its inhabitants, weave for us illusions, incompatible with the bustle of modern occupancy, and vanities of foolish present aristocracy. The same differ-

7. My italics.

8. "Blakesmoor" has been discussed and analyzed in a number of modern studies of Lamb: Daniel L. Mulcahy, "Charles Lamb: The Antithetical Manner and the Two Planes," 524–28; Fred. V. Randel, *The World of Elia: Charles Lamb's Essayistic Romanticism*, pp. 35–40; Robert D. Frank, *Don't Call me Gentle Charles!*, pp. 52–63; Monsman, pp. 138–44.

ence of feeling, I think, attends us between entering an empty and a crowded church. In the latter it is chance but some present human frailty — an act of inattention on the part of some of the auditory — or a trait of affectation, or worse, vain-glory, on that of the preacher — puts us by our best thoughts, disharmonizing the place and the occasion. But would'st thou know the beauty of holiness? — go alone on some week-day, borrowing the keys of good Master Sexton, traverse the cool aisles of some country church: think of the piety that has kneeled there — the congregations, old and young, that have found consolation there — the meek pastor — the docile parishioner. With no disturbing emotions, no cross conflicting comparisons, drink in the tranquillity of the place, till thou thyself become as fixed and motionless as the marble effigies that kneel and weep around thee.

After this prefatory paragraph of shared assumption about the emotional sustenance to be derived from a deserted building — all in keeping with the experience and the education provided for the reader by the initiating essays of the series — the drama of the essay begins with Elia's account of a journey to revisit such a building, "an old great house with which I had been impressed in this way in infancy." His experience is more radical and more threatening than anything to which the reader was earlier subjected. The question posed by the essay is, what happens to one's emotional and psychological life if the objects that called it into being no longer exist? To put it another way, would the reader's imaginative liberation in "The South-Sea House" have been possible without the physical building to provoke and to sustain it? Elia returns to Blakesmoor only to find its magnificence "crushed all at once into the mere dust and rubble . . ."

The anxiety created by this situation is revealed in the mounting grimness of tone of the succeeding brief paragraphs:

> The work of ruin had proceeded with a swift hand indeed, and the demolition of a few weeks had reduced it to — an antiquity.

> I was astonished at the indistinction of everything. Where had stood the great gates? What bounded the court-yard? Whereabout did the out-houses commence? a few bricks only lay as representatives of that which was so stately and so spacious.
>
> Death does not shrink up his human victim at this rate. The burnt ashes of a man weigh more in their proportion.

The next paragraph makes this anxiety even clearer as it enunciates the connection between the physical building and the speaker's internal life: "Had I seen these brick-and-mortar knaves at their process of destruction, at the plucking of every pannel I should have felt the varlets at my heart." Elia experiences two apparently conflicting reactions to the material loss of the object: a desire to have the material fact back; and a revelation, the consequences of which are as yet unrealized by him, that the house still exists in memory and in imagination.

> I should have cried out to them to spare a plank at least out of the cheerful store-room, in whose hot window-seat I used to sit and read Cowley, with the grass-plat before, and the hum and flappings of that one solitary wasp that ever haunted it about me — it is in mine ears now, as oft as summer returns; or a pannel of the yellow room.

It is from the persistence of the place in imagination and in memory that Elia in the course of the essay rebuilds it and re-captures the emotional strengths that accompanied its original possession. (It is not insignificant that at this point Elia calls for "planks" and "pannels," rather like a builder commencing his labors.)

The work of imaginative reconstruction now begins in earnest as "every plank and pannel" of the house is recalled and reassembled in the context of its emotional resonance for the responsive child:

> Why, every plank and pannel of that house for me had magic in it. The tapestried bed-rooms — tapestry so much better than painting — not adorning merely, but peopling the wainscots — at which childhood ever and anon would steal a

look, shifting its coverlid (replaced as quickly) to exercise its tender courage in a momentary eye-encounter with those stern bright visages, staring reciprocally — all Ovid on the walls, in colours vivider than his descriptions. Acteon in mid sprout, with the unappeasable prudery of Diana; and the still more provoking, and almost culinary coolness of Dan Phoebus, eel-fashion, deliberately divesting of Marsyas.

The Ovidian figures in memory are both subjects and objects of transformation. They dramatize transformation and aid in the gradual transformation of the house from its physical life (now threateningly vanished) to its "immortality" in the imagination and emotional life of Elia. The emotion the tapestried figures first provoked was an "exercise of tender courage." That "courage" in facing a threat is appropriately summoned up here, as the adult Elia searches anxiously for the sustenance now possibly lost with the destruction of the object that had originally inspired it.

Elia recalls next the child's confrontation with the ultimate threat — the extinction of all things in death:

> Then, that haunted room — in which old Mrs. Battle died — whereinto I have crept, but always in the daytime, with a passion of fear; and a sneaking curiosity, terror-tainted, to hold communication with the past. — *How shall they build it up again?*

Elia's present passion to recover the past, paralleling the child's, reaches its anxious height with the italicized exclamation. The referents for "*they*" and "*it*" are vague, a testimony to the speaker's disturbance. The "*it*" may be the house, the past, the strength of the child-Elia's imaginative power. Whatever it may be, the adult-Elia assumes someone else ("*they*") must reconstitute the nourishing source.

No "*they*" appears in answer to the despairing question: in the series of succeeding paragraphs, the work of reconstruction progresses with Elia himself, supported by memories. These memories focus less on the physical building than on the passionate and imaginative life of the child. Even the first of these

paragraphs, the most rich in exact physical details of the fur-
nishings of the house, reaches its climax with the statement:
"But I was a lonely child, and had the range at will of every
apartment, knew every nook and corner, wondered and worshipped everywhere." In the next paragraph, virtually everything is put in terms of the child's active emotional identification
with or coloration of the scene:

> The solitude of childhood is not so much the mother of
> thought, as it is the feeder of love, and silence, and admira-
> tion. So strange a passion for the place possessed me in those
> years, that, though there lay — I shame to say how few roods
> distant from the mansion — half hid by trees, what I judged
> some romantic lake, such was the spell which bound me to
> the house, and such my carefulness not to pass its strict and
> proper precincts, that the idle waters lay unexplored for me
> . . . . Variegated views, extensive prospects — and those at no
> great distance from the house — I was told of such — what
> were they to me, being out of the boundaries of my Eden? —
> So far from a wish to roam, I would have drawn, methought,
> still closer the fences of my chosen prison.

The child's very alienation by blood from the gentility of the
house simply called out his own instinct for gentility and thus
established his imaginative claim: "The claims of birth are ideal
merely," Elia now recognizes, "and what herald shall go about
to strip me of an idea? Is it trenchant to their swords? can it be
hacked off as a spur can? or torn away like a tarnished garter"?
The separation between child and adult and reader verbally disappears in Elia's acknowledgment of the timeless truth of the
child's behavior:

> What, else, were the families of the great to us? what
> pleasure should we take in their tedious genealogies, or their
> capitulatory brass monuments? What to us the uninterrupted
> current of their bloods, if our own did not answer within us
> to a cognate and correspondent elevation?

With this discovery of what constitutes true "gentility,"
namely, the activation of one's own noble feelings, Blakesmoor

is now addressed for the first time as alive. It lives now, as it did before for the child, by the very act of imaginatively possessing it:

> O wherefore else, O tattered and diminished 'Scutcheon that hung upon the time-worn walls of thy princely stairs, BLAKESMOOR! have I in childhood so oft stood poring upon thy mystic characters — thy emblematic supporters, with their prophetic "Resurgam" — till, every dreg of peasantry purging off, I received into myself Very Gentility? Thou wert first in my morning eyes; and of nights, hast detained my steps from bedward, till it was but a step from gazing at thee to dreaming on thee.
>
> This is the only true gentry by adoption; the veritable change of blood, and not, as empirics have fabled, by transfusion.

In a series of paragraphs each introduced by "mine," with mounting excitement Elia chronicles the child's total ownership of the place and at the same time dramatizes his own imaginative and emotional recovery of that experience: "Mine was the gallery of good old family portraits . . ."; "Mine, too, BLAKESMOOR, was thy noble Marble Hall," whose busts of the twelve Caesars came alive in the imagination of the child just as the figures in the family portraits "would seem to smile, reaching forward from the canvas, to recognize the new relationship."

In the next two paragraphs constituting the climax of this experience, "Mine" is repeated, but the verbs drop out as the child's possession becomes indistinguishable from the adult's: for example, "Mine, too, thy lofty Justice Hall. . . ." The penultimate paragraph now expands in its repossession to encompass the entire estate and to reach back in time, beyond even the Christian references at the start of the essay, to a deeper, more primitive and radically imaginative religious instinct:

> Mine too — whose else? — thy costly fruit-garden, with its sun-baked southern wall; the ampler pleasure-garden, rising backwards from the house in triple terraces, with flower-

> pots now of palest lead, save that a speck here and there, saved from the elements, bespake their pristine state to have been gilt and glittering; the verdant quarters backwarder still; and, stretching still beyond, in old formality, thy firry wilderness, the haunt of the squirrel, and the day-long murmuring wood-pigeon, with that antique image in the centre, God or Goddess I wist not; but child of Athens or old Rome never paid a sincerer worship to Pan or to Sylvanus in their native groves, than I to that fragmental mystery.

Initially, Elia had been disturbed that only a few bricks remained of Blakesmoor. Now the "fragmental" state of the presiding deity is worshipped, and appropriately so: the very fragmentation requires the imaginative exercise that constitutes true possession and internalization.

The final paragraph is divided into two sentences. The first — "Was it for this, that I kissed my childish hands too fervently in your idol worship, walks and windings of BLAKESMOOR! for this, or what sin of mine, has the plough passed over your pleasant places"? — raises the possible objection from conventional morality that the exercise of "pagan" imagination or some subsequent fall from innocence has provoked the loss of the object. But the final sentence answers with the fullness of faith that incorporates Christian values as well: "I sometimes think that as men, when they die, do not die all, so of their extinguished habitations there may be a hope — a germ to be revivified." A salvific remnant always endures in memory for the only immortality temporal man can know, the imaginative reconstruction of a nourishing past. This is what the child Elia had done; this is what the adult Elia has done in the course of the essay; and this is what the reader does with each encounter with the essay, an imaginative reliving of experience from the black-and-white "fragments" of paper and print.

3. MODES OF DISCOURSE
IN HAZLITT'S PROSE

"Words are a key to the affections." — Hazlitt, 1826

"When Hazlitt's interests as an essayist are compared with those of the great essayists of the past," John Kinnaird has observed,

> it is remarkable how traditional in orientation his work in the genre appears. Friendship, love, happiness, solitude, youth and age, duty, ambition, fame, travel, superstition, the fear of death — these and other perennial topics of the essay appear and reappear, and are most often addressed directly, not tangentially encountered as in Lamb.[1]

That is to say, Hazlitt's essays are texts of ideas; Lamb's are texts of character-revelation and dramatic self-discovery. Hazlitt's essays end either with conviction about a proposition or with the material and the stimulus for further exploration of that proposition; Lamb's end with the unfolding of internal strengths (and weaknesses) in Elia or in his reader.

Despite this difference, Hazlitt's essays are still closer to Lamb's writing than they are to Addison's "regular dissertations" in the *Spectator* or to the "scholastic method" of Johnson's *Rambler.*[2] *Their distinctiveness lies in Hazlitt's desire to achieve a particular engagement with the reader; from that desire stem craft and*

---

1. John Kinnaird, *William Hazlitt Critic of Power*, p. 272.
2. Hazlitt declared his preference for the *Tatler* over the *Spectator* because the "reflections" in the former "are less spun out into regular dissertations"; significantly, he adds, "something is left to the understanding of the reader" (*The Complete Works of William Hazlitt*, ed. P. P. Howe, vol. 4, 8). However, my reading of the *Tatler* reveals no anticipation of the specific rhetorical procedures, the dealings with the reader, found in a Hazlitt essay.

method. An analysis of a *Spectator* paper and a *Rambler* essay in terms of their contrasting dealings with the reader will make clear this distinctiveness.

Spectator 381 (17 May 1712)[3] served as a model of prose composition at Christ's Hospital in the 1790s;[4] it thus provides a good instance of an eighteenth-century tradition in which the romantic essayists had been trained but which, for all their admiration and respect, they were to transform so radically. The essay opens with a motto from Horace:

> *Aequam memento rebus in arduis*
> *Servare mentem non secus in bonis*
> *Ab insolenti temperatam*
> *Laetitia, moriture Deli.*

According to Addison's theory of mottoes, such quotations provide "some celebrated Thought upon [the topic], or a Thought of my own expressed in better Words, or some Similitude for the Illustration of my Subject"; in general, the employment of classical mottoes disarms the reader's apprehensions, "as it shews that [the writer] is supported by good Authorities, and is not singular in his Opinion."[5] Thus Addison begins, not asserting his difference from his reader's culture but emphasizing his alignment. The same effect is maintained throughout the essay in the easy switches from "I" to "we," with none of the strenuous maneuvering to join speaker and reader found in an Elia essay.

The first paragraph opens with the immediate statement of the proposition, "I have always preferred Chearfulness to Mirth," and continues:

3. All quotations from the *Spectator* papers are from the edition by Donald F. Bond, 5 vols. (Oxford University Press, 1965). For *Spectator* 381, see vol. 3, 429–32.

4. *The Autobiography of Leigh Hunt*, ed. J. E. Morpurgo, p. 79. Although he disliked the "moral and didactic tone of the Spectator," Hazlitt regarded "many of [the] moral Essays [as] exquisitely beautiful and quite happy," and specifically mentioned the one on "cheerfulness." See *Works of William Hazlitt*, vol. 6, 99.

5. *Spectator* 221, vol. 2, 358–61.

The latter I consider as an Act, the former as an Habit of the Mind. Mirth is short and transient, Chearfulness fixt and permanent. Those are often raised into the greatest Transports of Mirth, who are subject to the greatest Depressions of Melancholy. On the contrary, Chearfulness, tho' it does not give the Mind such an exquisite Gladness, prevents us from falling into any Depths of Sorrow. Mirth is like a Flash of Lightning that breaks thro' a gloom of Clouds, and glitters for a moment: Chearfulness keeps up a kind of Day-light in the Mind, and fills it with a steady and perpetual Serenity.

The rhetorical principle of this opening paragraph, indeed, of the entire essay, is contrast. Addison's treatment of his topic assumes clearly placed moral and intellectual opposites. (This should be kept in mind when we examine Hazlitt's elaborate essays of the 1820s, in which the contrasting elements are forever collapsing into each other and serving as syntheses for further refinements of the proposition, with further contrasts.) In addition, the meaning of the initial proposition remains fixed throughout the paragraph and the essay. (In Hazlitt, the proposition is being continually re-examined.) Finally, the similitude that announces the conclusion of this introductory paragraph is illustrative rather than constitutive; that is, it consolidates the argumentation thus far rather than advancing it. (Again, the difference in Hazlitt's use of figures will be significant.)

In the succeeding two paragraphs, Addison's preference for "chearfulness" over mirth is supported with the opinions and the examples of moral authorities. The first is devoted to the limitations of mirth; the second, in contrast, describes the values of "chearfulness":

Men of austere Principles look upon Mirth as too wanton and dissolute for a state of Probation, and as fill'd with a certain Triumph and Insolence of Heart, that is inconsistent with a Life which is every moment obnoxious to the greatest Dangers. Writers of this Complexion have observed, that the Sacred Person who was the great Pattern of Perfection was never seen to Laugh.

> Chearfulness of Mind is not liable to any of these Excep-
> tions; it is of a serious and composed Nature, it does not throw
> the Mind into a Condition improper for the present State of
> Humanity, and is very conspicuous in the Characters of those
> who are look'd upon as the greatest Philosophers among the
> Heathens, as well as among those who have been deservedly
> esteemed as Saints and Holy Men among Christians.

The vocabulary throughout is general, even abstract. The reader
is involved in a relationship of intellectual concepts, not in an
imaginatively charged world of sensory images, personal experience, or metaphoric expression.

With careful symmetry, following these three introductory
paragraphs, which state the proposition and support it with authorities, Addison devotes three paragraphs to the proof of the
proposition with the classical topos of "consequences." The first
paragraph defines the consequences in relation to ourselves;
the second in our relations to other men; and the third in our
relations to God. The next six paragraphs are devoted to the
"causes" of "chearfulness." The exposition is divided between
what obstructs and what promotes this quality, thus preserving
the cause-and-effect logic of the entire essay, as well as the all-
pervasive rhetorical tactic of contrast. The first paragraph
defines "the Sense of Guilt" as an obstruction, the second
"Atheism." The latter paragraph clearly illustrates the easy
identification of reader and author, who share moral assumptions, experience, and respect for classical example:

> There is something so particularly gloomy and offensive to
> Human Nature in the Prospect of Non-Existence, that I can-
> not but wonder, with many Excellent Writers, how it is pos-
> sible for a Man to outlive the Expectation of it. For my own
> part, I think the Being of a God is so little to be doubted, that
> it is almost the only Truth we are sure of, and such a Truth as
> we meet with in every Object, in every Occurrence, and in
> every Thought.

The third and fourth paragraphs of this middle section
draw together the two sources of obstruction in a summary

statement, rule out all other sources, and mark a close in argumentation with an illustrative similitude: "The tossing of a Tempest does not discompose him, which he is sure will bring him to a Joyful Harbour." In contrast, the next two paragraphs describe what promotes cheerfulness in a man of "Virtue and Right Reason": "The Consideration of his own Nature" and "of that Being on whom he has a Dependance." These paragraphs, in effect, answer the obstructions of sin and atheism. A virtuous man can rejoice in the knowledge of his eternal identity and accordingly in the prospect of an increasing progress toward moral perfection and happiness; in support of this, his belief in God contains the recognition that "we depend upon a Being . . . whose Goodness and Truth engage him to make those happy who desire it of him, and whose Unchangeableness will secure us in this Happiness to all Eternity."

Appropriately for an essay held together by a structure of causes-and-effects and contrasts, the concluding paragraph summarizes the entire essay in these terms:

> Such Considerations, which every one should perpetually cherish in his Thoughts, will banish from us all that secret Heaviness of Heart, which unthinking Men are subject to when they lie under no real Affliction, all that Anguish which we may feel from any Evil that actually oppresses us, to which I may likewise add those little Cracklings of Mirth and Folly that are apter to betray Virtue than support it; and establish in us such an even and chearful Temper, as makes us pleasant to our selves, to those with whom we converse, and to him whom we were made to please.

The conclusiveness of the argument is revealed by the complete incorporation of the reader into this summary affirmation of the proposition.

Rambler 150 (24 August 1751)[6] opens with a classical quotation from Lucan that states judiciously the moral point of this

---

6. All quotations are from the text edited by W. J. Bate and Albrecht B. Strauss, in *The Yale Edition of the Works of Samuel Johnson* (New Haven-London: Yale University Press, 1958-), 5, 32–37.

essay on the uses of adversity: "*O munera nonꝺum/ Intellecta Deum!*" Like the *Spectator* paper, Johnson's essay also engages the reader in a discursive process. The opening paragraph (one complex sentence) employs the logic of cause and effect in multiple ways. The initial dependent clause embodies in itself such a process:

> As daily experience makes it evident that misfortunes are unavoidably incident to human life, that calamity will neither be repelled by fortitude, nor escaped by flight, neither awed by greatness, nor eluded by obscurity;

The same clause serves as the evidence for the conclusion found in the main clause: "philosophers have endeavoured to reconcile us to that condition which they cannot teach us to mend. . . ." There follows a representation of the argument of these philosophers, which is also put in terms of cause and effect:

> by persuading us that most of our evils are made afflictive only by ignorance or perverseness, and that nature has annexed to every vicissitude of external circumstances, some advantage sufficient to overbalance all its inconveniences.

As is customary in *Rambler* essays, the second paragraph initiates the discourse of the essay by calling into question the truth of the received opinion:

> This attempt [by philosophers] may perhaps be justly suspected of resemblance to the practice of physicians, who when they cannot mitigate pain, destroy sensibility, and endeavour to conceal by opiates the inefficacy of their other medicines.

The succeeding paragraph, in partial answer to this objection, asserts the general pragmatic value of the received opinion, again in terms of effects: "The antidotes with which philosophy has medicated the cup of life, though they cannot give it salubrity and sweetness, have at least allayed its bitterness, and contempered its malignity." The next paragraph continues the exposition of the value of this opinion; however, the benevolent effects thus far are rather negative: our distress is reduced but not completely removed. Johnson now cites the positive opinion of an authority (Seneca) that misfortune is "necessary to the pleasures of the mind." This opinion in turn must be examined and proved if the proposition of the essay is to stand conclusively.

The examination begins with the premise that "curiosity is in great and generous minds the first passion and the last," a premise developed and supported with the classical example of Jason's incitement of the young Acastus. The next step is to prove that the gratification of such noble curiosity requires adversity, and therefore adversity is to be welcomed. Johnson phrases this in the deduction:

> If therefore it is to be proved that distress is necessary to the attainment of knowledge, and that a happy situation hides from us so large a part of the field of meditation, the envy of many who repine at the sight of affluence and splendor will be much diminished.

The proof of Seneca's contention that distress is necessary to the attainment of knowledge follows in a three-part exposition of cause and effect: (1) distress is necessary to rejoice truly in our experience, to have "a just sense of better fortune"; (2) for knowledge of our own strengths and weaknesses, opposition and difficulties are indispensable; and (3) "some variety of fortune" is necessary for understanding "the manners, principles and affections" of other men. This completes the proof, and the essay immediately and appropriately closes.

Johnson's essay, like Addison's, assumes an engagement with the reader primarily, indeed almost exclusively, in terms of his response to a logical process.[7] The situation is quite different

---

7. Needless to say, there are other kinds of eighteenth-century essay-writing than the more formal *Spectator* and *Rambler* examples here analyzed.

in a Hazlitt essay, even in an early one like "On the Love of the Country," which originally appeared in the "Round Table" section of Leigh Hunt's *Examiner* on 27 November 1814, and was collected in the *Round Table* volumes of 1817.[8]

A difference is evident at first glance. There is no classical motto to suggest the ancient authorities supporting the writer's opinions; moreover, the essay in its *Round Table* text is cast in the form of a letter, emphasizing still more the personal and possibly idiosyncratic nature of the discourse to follow. Indeed, the opening sentence specifically defines the originality of the point of view:

> I do not know that any one has ever explained satisfactorily the true source of our attachment to natural objects, or of that soothing emotion which the sight of the country hardly ever fails to infuse into the mind.

The rest of the paragraph rules out various explanations offered by others and announces Hazlitt's intention to explain "a more general principle, which has been left untouched." Where Johnson sought to examine and to reaffirm a traditional opinion, Hazlitt announces a new one.

Still another difference in procedure is evident with the second paragraph initiating the first of the two steps in Hazlitt's exposition of his proposition, which is as yet not stated. We are given an authoritative example *before* the proposition; in short, an active induction is under way. The personalism of Hazlitt's approach is also maintained in the very choice of example, the self-consciously subjective evidence of Rousseau's *Confessions*:

(Predecessors to the romantic familiar essay have been explored by: Marie H. Law, *The English Familiar Essay in the Early Nineteenth-century*; and Melvin R. Watson, *Magazine Serials and the Essay Tradition 1746–1820*.) However, it was these two illustrious examples that the romantic writers regularly cited in defining their own quite differently conceived prose ventures.

8. I follow the 1817 text in *Works of Hazlitt*, vol. 4, 17–21. The style of "On the Love of the Country" has been closely analyzed as a contrast to Johnson's by W. K. Wimsatt, Jr., *The Prose Style of Samuel Johnson* (New Haven: Yale University Press, 1941).

Rousseau, in his Confessions, (the most valuable of all his works), relates, that when he took possession of his room at Annecy, at the house of his beloved mistress and friend, he found that he could see "a little spot of green" from his window, which endeared his situation the more to him, because, he says, it was the first time he had had this object constantly before him since he left Boissy, the place where he was at school when a child.

Only then is the first part of the proposition announced:

Were it not for the recollections habitually associated with them, natural objects could not interest the mind in the manner they do.

What follows on this is not the positive proof expected in the Addisonian or Johnsonian examples. Instead, Hazlitt devotes the rest of the paragraph to the *inversion* of the proposition, developing that inversion with resonant images and an extended poetic quotation:

No doubt, the sky is beautiful; the clouds sail majestically along its bosom; the sun is cheering; there is something exquisitely graceful in the manner in which a plant or tree puts forth its branches; the motion with which they bend and tremble in the evening breeze is soft and lovely; there is music in the babbling of a brook; the view from the top of a mountain is full of grandeur; nor can we behold the ocean with indifference. Or, as the Minstrel sweetly sings —
"Oh how can'st thou renounce the boundless store
Of charms which Nature to her votary yields!
The warbling woodland, the resounding shore,
The pomp of groves, the garniture of fields;
All that the genial ray of morning gilds,
And all that echoes to the song of even,
All that the mountain's sheltering bosom shields,
And all the dread magnificence of heaven,
Oh how can'st thou renounce, and hope to be forgiven!"

It is only in the next paragraph that the affirmative proof of the proposition — the pleasures of nature depend on association—is developed. What are we to make of this procedure? Hazlitt apparently wants the reader to participate in the argumentative process by imaginatively living through the powerful opposing evidence; he is not concerned to set down, in a neat order of cause and effect, the deductions leading to the proof of his proposition.

The second point in the exposition, "the transferable nature of our feelings with respect to physical objects," is now introduced. This point also draws on highly personal experience:

> I remember when I was abroad, the trees, and grass, and wet leaves, rustling in the walks of the Thuilleries, seemed to me as much English, to be as much the same trees and grass, that I had always been used to, as the sun shining over my head was the same sun which I saw in England; the faces only were foreign to me. Whence comes this difference?

The answer is directly stated:

> It arises from our always imperceptibly connecting the idea of the individual with man, and only the idea of the class with natural objects. In the one case, the external appearance or physical structure is the least thing to be attended to; in the other, it is every thing.

The evidence or proof of this position is superficially like the cause-and-effect connections of Johnsonian discourse; for example, a "therefore" announces a logical deduction of previous statements. However, the effect of argument here depends as much on Hazlitt's presenting the experience of his own mind moving through the evidence as it does on our awareness of the evidence-conclusion relationship:

> The springs that move the human form, and make it friendly or adverse to me, lie hid within it. There is an infinity of motives, passions, and ideas, contained in that narrow compass, of which I know nothing, and in which I have no share. Each individual is a world to himself, governed by a thousand contradictory and wayward impulses. I can, therefore, make no inference from one individual to another; nor can my habit-

ual sentiments, with respect to any individual, extend beyond himself to others.

As he turns to the other term in his contrast, Hazlitt uses stylistic rather than logical tactics to develop the point; here the reader is presented with argument through personification:

> But it is otherwise with respect to Nature. There is neither hypocrisy, caprice, nor mental reservation in her favours. Our intercourse with her is not liable to accident or change, interruption or disappointment. She smiles on us still the same.

This in turn is followed by an "instance from which one conclusion ("Hence") after another ("Hence") deductively follows, but it is again the mind's experiencing the discursive process that occupies Hazlitt:

> Thus, to give an obvious instance, if I have once enjoyed the cool shade of a tree, and been lulled into a deep repose by the sound of a brook running at its feet, I am sure that wherever I can find a tree and a brook, I can enjoy the same pleasure again. Hence, when I imagine these objects, I can easily form a mystic personification of the friendly power that inhabits them, Dryad or Naiad, offering its cool fountain or its tempting shade. Hence the origin of the Grecian mythology.

The generalization that follows this is itself a description of a mental action in which "we" engage.

> All objects of the same kind being the same, not only in their appearance, but in their practical uses, we habitually confound them together under the same general idea; and, whatever fondness we may have conceived for one, is immediately placed to the common account.

A logical consequence of this is then presented, quite in the spirit of Johnson or Addison:

> It is this circumstance which gives that refinement, expansion, and wild interest to feelings of this sort, when strongly

excited, which every one must have experienced who is a true lover of Nature.

However, this deduction is followed by an extended passage of lyrical prose illustrating the general statement, a passage that is quite without parallel in the eighteenth-century models we have examined. The passage indeed illustrates the generalization, but the extent of the passage and its climactic location in the essay make it more than a simple example; Hazlitt obviously intended it as the cumulative "proof" of the proposition for the reader, a proof carried out in poetic quotations and literal and figurative images, by which "we" are incited to second an experience with nature that begins with the "I":

> The sight of the setting sun does not affect me so much from the beauty of the object itself, from the glory kindled through the glowing skies, the rich broken columns of light, or the dying streaks of day, as that it indistinctly recalls to me numberless thoughts and feelings with which, through many a year and season, I have watched his bright descent in the warm summer evenings, or beheld him struggling to cast a "farewell sweet" through the thick clouds of winter. I love to see the trees first covered with leaves in the spring, the primroses peeping out from some sheltered bank, and the innocent lambs running races on the soft green turf; because, at that birth-time of Nature, I have always felt sweet hopes and happy wishes — which have not been fulfilled! The dry reeds rustling on the side of the stream, — the woods swept by the loud blast, — the dark massy foliage of autumn, — the grey trunks and naked branches of the trees in winter, — the sequestered copse and wide extended heath, — the warm sunny showers, and December snows, — have all charms for me; there is no object, however trifling or rude, that has not, in some mood or other, found the way to my heart; and I might say, in the words of the poet,
> "To me the meanest flower that blows can give
> Thoughts that do often lie too deep for tears."
> Thus Nature is a kind of universal home, and every object it presents to us an old acquaintance with unaltered looks.

— —"Nature did ne'er betray
The heart that lov'd her, but through all the years
Of this our life, it is her privilege
To lead from joy to joy."
For there is that consent and mutual harmony among all her
works, one undivided spirit pervading them throughout,
that, if we have once knit ourselves in hearty fellowship to
any of them, they will never afterwards appear as strangers
to us, but, which ever way we turn, we shall find a secret
power to have gone out before us, moulding them into such
shapes as fancy loves, informing them with life and sympathy, bidding them put on their festive looks and gayest at-
tire at our approach, and to pour all their sweets and choicest
treasures at our feet. For him, then, who has well acquainted
himself with Nature's works, she wears always one face, and
speaks the same well-known language, striking on the heart,
amidst unquiet thoughts and the tumult of the world, like the
music of one's native tongue heard in some far off country.

The final paragraph is a quiet coda to the essay, which has
really been completed with the burst of poetic quotation, personal reminiscences, and sustained personification of the paragraph before. Hazlitt merely extends the point to the effect of
man-made objects (cottages, churches, etc.) in the natural
scene. There is no summary of the argument as in Addison, no
continuation and completion of formal logical proof as in
Johnson. Although throughout the essay logical connections
are being made and the larger organization is divided into the
exposition of two points that explain Hazlitt's idea "On the
Love of the Country," still the rhetoric of the essay is constantly
working away from a strictly logical response. Even in as early
an effort as this essay, Hazlitt's already considerable resources
as a writer are devoted to making the reader either the witness
to or the participant in the process of arriving at a truth.

Within the general experiential mode of Hazlitt's prose, the
particular structures of discourse found in individual essays are
enormously varied, as further examples from *The Round Table*
reveal. "On Poetical Versatility," for example, depends on sys-

tematic verbal patterning as a way of structuring its discourse. This paragraph-essay[9] begins with an initial paradoxical statement: "The spirit of poetry is in itself favourable to humanity and liberty; but, we suspect, not when its aid is most wanted." The rest of the essay clarifies and proves this, in two stages. First, poetry being an unearthly force is inevitably damaged when it is involved with worldly matters. Second, in addition to its unique nature being damaged by such contact, poetry does damage to freedom and humanity by its contact with such matters.

The two stages of explanation are most carefully and self-consciously marked off and expanded. "The spirit of poetry" or "poetry" or the pronoun "it" dominates the presentation of the first point; every one of the first ten sentences begins with one of these three words:

> *The spirit of poetry* is not the spirit of mortification or of martyrdom. *Poetry* dwells in a perpetual Utopia of its own, and is for that reason very ill calculated to make a Paradise upon earth, by encountering the shocks and disappointments of the world. *Poetry*, like law, is a fiction, only a more agreeable one. *It* does not create difficulties where they do not exist; but contrives to get rid of them, whether they exist or not. *It* is not entangled in cobwebs of its own making, but soars above all obstacles. *It* cannot be "constrained by mastery."[10]

In addition to the control achieved by initial words, this section also has a calculated development; it moves through negative statements and a contrast with the law to reach a climax, in the immediately succeeding lines, with an extended constitutive metaphor of poetry as an aerial being:

> It has the range of the universe; it traverses the empyrean, and looks down on nature from a higher sphere. When it

9. This was originally a paragraph in the *Examiner* essay of 22 December 1816, "Illustrations of the Times Newspaper — on Modern Lawyers and Poets." I follow the 1817 text in *Works of Hazlitt*, vol. 4, 151–53.

10. My italics here and in the next paragraph.

lights upon the earth, it loses some of its dignity and its use. Its strength is in its wings; its element the air. Standing on its feet, jostling with the crowd, it is liable to be overthrown, trampled on, and defaced; for its wings are of a dazzling brightness, "heaven's own tint," and the least soil upon them shews to disadvantage.

The second part of the paragraph-essay is likewise held together verbally. In this case, almost every sentence begins with "poets," the active earthly agents of damage-doing:

> *Poets* live in an ideal world, where they make every thing out according to their wishes and fancies. *They* either find things delightful or make them so. *They* feign the beautiful and grand out of their own minds, and imagine all things to be, not what they are, but what they ought to be.

This sustained emphasis on the agents of damage is continued until the end. Just as the first part of the paragraph moved toward a climax in the form of an extended metaphor, so the second part is not simply an accumulation of "they" clauses; it is controlled by a tonal change moving more and more to a hostile view of poets. As the lines just quoted indicate, poets are initially described in the second part like the aerial beings of the first part. However, toward the end we read:

> Poets . . . cannot do well without sympathy and flattery. . . . They do not like to be shut out when laurels are to be given away at Court — or places under Government to be disposed of, in romantic situations in the country. They are happy to be reconciled on the first opportunity to prince and people, and to exchange their principles for a pension. . . . Truth alone does not satisfy their pampered appetites without the sauce of praise.

The first part of the paragraph elevates poetry in describing it as a free-spirited being, in that sense fulfilling the first half of the initiating paradox of the essay, that "the spirit of poetry is in itself favourable to humanity and liberty." The second part moves to the description of poets as creatures of "pampered appetites," loose principles, and political expediency, thus illustrating the second half of the paradox — when its aid is most wanted, in times when liberty is most endangered, poetry (in the hands of poets) turns out not to be "favourable."

This is not, of course, a complete analysis of the paragraph. One could note the perfect *isocolon* at one place, the *antimetabole* at another, the admirable balance of clauses and ideas; and the sense of finality achieved at the end, as the last sentence ("Milton was, however, a poet, and an honest man; he was Cromwell's secretary") brings us down abruptly from the generalizations and the frequent high rhetoric of everything else before. All I am concerned about is demonstrating the very deliberate use of style with all its affective and rhetorical possibilities, rather than formal logic, as the vehicle of exposition.

A different mode of organization and development is found in the essay "On Actors and Acting,"[11] which immediately follows "On Poetical Versatility" in the *Round Table* volumes. The major revisions that Hazlitt made in transferring the essay from the *Examiner* are important as indicators of his artistic craft. In its original version, the essay illustrated that casual order of topics for which Hazlitt is frequently criticized. It consisted of three paragraphs. After some light-hearted remarks about the insubstantiality of actors,

> players are "the abstracts and brief chronicles of the time";
> the motley representatives of human nature. . . . To-day
> kings, to-morrow beggars, it is only when they are themselves, that they are nothing. . . . Their very thoughts are not
> their own,

the first paragraph describes the stage as "a school of instruction" in manners and morals. The second paragraph describes the stage as a "source of amusement" both in the performance

11. This is the first of two essays with that title which originally appeared in the *Examiner* on 5 January 1817. I follow the *Round Table* text in *Works of Hazlitt*, vol. 4, 153–56.

and as a subject for conversation afterward. The third describes the stage as a source of acquaintance with former times. I call this order casual, for there is no reason why the order might not be reversed or interchanged. Indeed, Hazlitt seems to avoid the expected climactic order of moving toward the topic of greatest conventional value — moral instruction.

When he revised the essay, Hazlitt added a final paragraph describing the playgoer's feelings on John Bannister's retirement from the stage. He also divided the original third paragraph into two paragraphs: the first merely asserts that the stage gives us the experience of past times, with some examples of the range of past times revived; the second focuses this in an intimate way by dwelling on our personal affection for a particular actor (John Kemble) because he has given us this pleasure in the past. This intimacy and these bonds of affection are expanded in the new final paragraph on Bannister's retirement, which opens:

> One of the most affecting things we know is to see a favourite actor take leave of the stage. We were present not long ago when Mr. Bannister quitted it. We do not wonder that his feelings were overpowered on the occasion; ours were nearly so too.

It is the very intimacy now achieved that makes the retirement so affecting, and so serious. As Hazlitt declares in the final two sentences of the paragraph,

> It glances a mortifying reflection on the shortness of human life, and the vanity of human pleasures. Something reminds us, that "all the world's a stage, and all the men and women merely players."

With this, Hazlitt achieves a circularity of structure. The essay opens with a Shakespearean quotation ("Players are 'the abstracts and brief chronicles of the time'") and closes with one as well. The conclusion returns to reinforce, now in a more personal and heartfelt way, the original topic of the stage as "the best teacher of morals, for it is the truest and most intelligible picture of life." The insubstantiality of the actors, their lack of reality, had been a light touch at the opening of the essay; by the final sentence, the insubstantiality has been extended to all of us. The first paragraph had emphasized the strictly ethical side of the theater's moral instruction; for example, it had affirmed that a production of *The Beggar's Opera* puts down the practice of highway robbery. The ending of the revised version moves to a much deeper moral lesson and the ultimate truth of life — the transience of all human experience and endeavors. The path between these two positions is a carefully contrived identification of reader-audience with actors that opens out the final perception.

It is perhaps to be expected that the emphasis and the procedures revealed in the *Round Table* essays would continue in the later familiar or informal essays of *Table-Talk* and *The Plain Speaker*, as well as in the "character essays" of the *Spirit of the Age*. But even when Hazlitt's intentions were most obviously didactic, as in his discussion "Of Poetry in General" in *The Lectures on the English Poets* (1818), the same tactics were employed. A good example is the long third paragraph of that discussion, which attempts to explain the "subject-matter" of poetry through three definitions developed in the course of the paragraph. In order of appearance, these are: (1) "Poetry is the language of the imagination and the passions"; (2) "Poetry is the universal language which the heart holds with nature and itself"; and (3) "Poetry is that fine particle within us, that expands, rarifies, refines, raises our whole being: without it 'man's life is poor as beast's.'"[12]

There is an obvious movement from the abstraction of the first definition, through the personification of the second definition, to the very framing of the final definition in terms of "our" possession of that redeeming instinct. Thus, as he progressively

12. *Works of Hazlitt*, vol. 5, 1–2. See David Bromwich's *Hazlitt: The Mind of a Critic*, pp. 252–54, for a discussion of the fifth paragraph, which raises some of the same problems of definition.

clarifies his definition, Hazlitt attempts to identify that "subject-matter" with his reader. (It should be noted also that as he moves from definition to definition the language becomes more technically poetic, so that with the final clarification Hazlitt literally quotes poetry and uses alliteration in his prose.)

As preparation for the final definition that conclusively acknowledges all of "us" as poets and the "subject-matter" of poetry as "our" internal life, Hazlitt rules out various objections to, or false conceptions of, poetry that would separate it from a central position in our affective experience; for, he declares, "all that is worth remembering in life, is the poetry of it." A contrast with history is also used to establish the greater human relevance of poetry: history records "the empty cases in which the affairs of the world are packed," but "there is no thought or feeling that can have entered into the mind of man . . . that is not a fit subject for poetry."

In an extended criticism of the *Lectures* in the *Quarterly Review*,[13] E. S. Barrett and William Gifford charged this particular paragraph with "extravagance" and "legerdemain" for its use of the term "poetry" in three distinct senses: the contrast with history refers to poetry as written composition; "all that is worth remembering in life, is the poetry of it" pertains strictly to the subject-matter of these compositions; and the final definition, "Poetry is the fine particle within us," describes the state of mind or faculty producing poetry. There is some justice to these charges. Certainly the discriminations between these three quite different meanings are not clearly marked for the reader and are, in fact, rather blurred. But it is precisely the strategy of the paragraph to make this blurring and thus to end the separation between a verse-composition with its particular subject matter and the reader's own profoundly poetic nature. In direct response to these charges Hazlitt acknowledged the three distinct meanings but argued that he had used them to find their common quality, which was an experience of the reader's own

13. *Quarterly Review* 19 (July 1818), 424–34.

psychological life: "a movement of imagination in the mind" caused by "an unusual vividness in external objects or in our immediate impressions . . . leading by natural association or sympathy to harmony of sound and the modulation of verse in expressing it."[14] All the rhetorical art of the "prose" paragraph had been directed to creating this "poetic" experience.

The works we have analyzed thus far were intended to bring the reader to clear comprehension of an expository point; for all their rhetorical and verbal subtlety, they ended with a sense of finality and completion. In the longer essays of the 1820s, however, Hazlitt is more often interested in exposing the reader to a play of possibilities around a central idea, the "dramatic contrast and ironical point of view to which the whole is subjected,"[15] as he admiringly described the procedures of his eighteenth-century predecessors at their best. The very titles ("On Genius and Common Sense," "On Paradox and Commonplace," "On Londoners and Country People," "On Vulgarity and Affectation") indicate that Hazlitt is examining two contrasting perspectives. As a reading of the essays indicates, there is no necessary attempt at resolution or reconciliation; the reader is left unsettled, curious, and still engaged with the subject. "On Going a Journey" (1822)[16] reveals the elaborate dialectic game to which the reader is frequently subjected in these mature essays.

The opening paragraph immediately establishes polarities between traveling alone and traveling with others. The polari-

14. *A Letter to William Gifford, Esq.* (1819), in *Works of Hazlitt*, vol. 9, 44–45.

15. *Works of Hazlitt*, vol. 6, 95. For valuable commentary of the differences between the earlier and later Hazlitt essays in these terms, see Kinnaird, pp. 275–80.

16. Originally published in *The New Monthly Magazine* (January 1822), the essay was included in the second volume of *Table-Talk* of that year and in the subsequent editions of 1824 and 1825. Howe's text (vol. 8, 181–89) incorporates the revisions of these later editions. For a recent extensive analysis of "On Going a Journey," see W. P. Albrecht, "Structure in Two of Hazlitt's Essays," 181–90. Robert Ready deals with the essay in a more summary fashion in his critical study of the *Table-Talk* volumes, *Hazlitt at Table*.

ties are apparently happily resolved when the perfect society is achieved in isolation:

> One of the pleasantest things in the world is going a journey; but I like to go by myself. I can enjoy society in a room; but out of doors, nature is company enough for me. I am then never less alone than when alone.

Never again will the opposing points of view be so happily accommodated; and this brief short paragraph, in contrast to the long complex paragraphs to follow, is in effect a setting up of expectations in the reader that will be constantly reversed and unsettled as the essay continues.

Hazlitt's separation from society — and supposedly from his reader — to achieve "perfect" society is even more pronounced at the start of the succeeding paragraph:

> I cannot see the wit of walking and talking at the same time. When I am in the country, I wish to vegetate like the country. I am not for criticising hedge-rows and black cattle. I go out of town in order to forget the town and all that is in it. There are those who for this purpose go to watering-places, and carry the metropolis with them. I like more elbow-room, and fewer incumbrances. I like solitude, when I give myself up to it, for the sake of solitude; nor do I ask for
> — "a friend in my retreat,
> Whom I may whisper solitude is sweet."

But this radical "separation" immediately turns into a shared experience: "The soul of a journey is liberty; perfect liberty, to think, feel, do just as one pleases. We go a journey chiefly to be free of all impediments and of all inconveniences; to leave ourselves behind, much more to get rid of others." At this point a new society or at least a new relationship is attempted to be forged between reader and writer as we, too, are asked to shed "our" false social selves.

The paradoxical process by which the speaker initially liberated himself is repeated. At the start of the second paragraph, the "I" wished to "vegetate like the country," to leave talk, criticism, thought; but soon he writes: "Give me the clear blue sky over my head, and the green turf beneath my feet, a winding road before me, and a three hours' march to dinner — and then to thinking!" Just as earlier a separation from society was necessary for the achievement of the perfect society, so absence of one kind of thought is necessary for the achievement of true thought. The shedding of the speaker's ordinary self and thought soon climaxes with the repossession of the true self and the paradox of silence as "perfect eloquence":

> I laugh, I run, I leap, I sing for joy. From the point of yonder rolling cloud, I plunge into my past being, and revel there, as the sunburnt Indian plunges headlong into the wave that wafts him to his native shore. Then long-forgotten things, like "sunken wrack and sumless treasuries," burst upon my eager sight, and I begin to feel, think, and be myself again. Instead of an awkward silence, broken by attempts at wit or dull common-places, mine is that undisturbed silence of the heart which alone is perfect eloquence.

And just as earlier, the liberation of the "I" from the restraints of the "you" turns into the liberation of the "you":

> I have just now other business in hand, which would seem idle to you, but is with me "the very stuff of the conscience." Is not this wild rose sweet without a comment? Does not this daisy leap to my heart, set in its coat of emerald? Yet if I were to explain to you the circumstance that has so endeared it to me, you would only smile. Had I not better then keep it to myself, and let it serve me to brood over, from here to yonder craggy point, and from thence onward to the far-distant horizon? I should be but bad company all that way, and therefore prefer being alone, I have heard it said that you may, when the moody fit comes on, walk or ride on by yourself, and indulge your reveries. But this looks like a breach of manners, a neglect of others, and you are thinking all the time that you ought to rejoin your party.

The converging identities and experiences of the "I" and "you" as each achieves his freedom become even clearer several lines later: "I like to have it all my own way; but this is impossible unless you are alone, or in such company as I do not covet." The convergence has been brought about by nondiscursive procedures, whose frustration of the structure of logic and deduction is the avenue as well as the illustration of the reader's achievement of freedom.

The accomplishment of this union, and also a remaining challenge to the union, is evident in the "I"-"you"-"we" pattern of the following passage still from the same paragraph:

> Now I never quarrel with myself, and take all my own conclusions for granted till I find it necessary to defend them against objections. It is not merely that you may not be of accord on the objects and circumstances that present themselves before you — they may recall a number of ideas, and lead to associations too delicate and refined to be possibly communicated to others. Yet these I love to cherish, and sometimes still fondly clutch them, when I can escape from the throng to do so. To give way to our feelings before company, seems extravagance or affectation; on the other hand, to have to unravel this mystery of our being at every turn, and to make others take an equal interest in it (otherwise the end is not answered) is a task to which few are competent. We must "give it an understanding, but no tongue."

A secure union of "I" and reader has been achieved. But how can one both experience and explain the deepest responses on a journey to those who do not immediately share them? A level of discourse, beyond even the rich rhetoric of the essay thus far, is needed. Such discourse is identified with the genius of Coleridge and the language of poetry, here illustrated by a passage of natural description from Fletcher's *Faithful Shepherdess*. Hazlitt comments:

> Had I words and images at command like these, I would attempt to wake the thoughts that lie slumbering on golden ridges in the evening clouds: but at the sight of nature my fancy, poor as it is, droops and closes up its leaves, like flowers at sunset.

Thus this paragraph, for all its achievement, ends on a note of incompleteness: "I must have time to collect myself," Hazlitt concludes, as he falls back into isolation. A firmer bridge of discourse between the liberated self and the rest of the world is to be sought.

For the accomplishment of this, a reentry into society is appropriate, but it must be one that does not compromise the self. This reentry is provided by an inn, a half-way house between the freedom of the self achieved in the journey and the identity imposed by normative society. An encounter with a stranger at an inn enables us to be in society and yet

> to lose our importunate, tormenting, everlasting personal identity in the elements of nature, and become the creature of the moment, clear of all ties. . . . We baffle prejudice and disappoint conjecture; and from being so to others, begin to be objects of curiosity and wonder even to ourselves.

An inn is associated for Hazlitt with one of the most significant, indeed almost apocalyptic, days of his life, his twentieth birthday on 10 April 1798. The circumstances and feelings of that day represented the greatest possibility Hazlitt ever experienced for the union of all men. Even in memory it inspires the resonant poetic discourse that was sought earlier and that is required for the communication of our deepest responses. Significantly, the following passage includes quotations from Coleridge, who was earlier hailed as the genius of that discourse:

> It was on the tenth of April, 1798, that I sat down to a volume of the New Eloise, at the inn at Llangollen, over a bottle of sherry and a cold chicken. The letter I chose was that in which St. Preux describes his feelings as he first caught a glimpse from the heights of the Jura of the Pays de Vaud, which I had brought with me as a *bonne bouche* to crown the evening with. It was my birth-day, and I had for the first time come from a place in the neighbourhood to visit this delightful spot. The road to Llangollen turns off between Chirk and Wrexham; and on passing a certain point, you come all at once upon the valley, which opens like an amphitheatre,

broad, barren hills rising in majestic state on either side, with "green upland swells that echo to the bleat of flocks" below, and the river Dee dabbling over its stony bed in the midst of them. The valley at this time "glittered green with sunny showers," and a budding ash-tree dipped its tender branches in the chiding stream. How proud, how glad I was to walk along the high road that commanded the delicious prospect, repeating the lines which I have just quoted from Mr. Coleridge's poems! But besides the prospect which opened beneath my feet, another also opened to my inward sight, a heavenly vision, on which were written, in letters large as Hope could make them, these four words, LIBERTY, GENIUS, LOVE, VIRTUE; which have since faded into the light of common day, or mock my idle gaze.

As the last sentence sadly indicates, the promise of 1798 was never achieved. Thus, Hazlitt is again plunged into isolation, severed from the hopeful expansive self of that consecrated time. However, at the conclusion of this magnificent paragraph, Hazlitt reaffirms in Wordsworthian and biblical cadence that the promise of his youth, however betrayed, is still the hoped-for goal:

Yet will I turn to thee in thought, O sylvan Dee, as then thou wert, in joy, in youth and gladness; and thou shalt always be to me the river of Paradise, where I will drink of the waters of life freely!

Thus the tension of the essay remains, and the reader stays undetermined and unsettled.

The succeeding paragraph, though stated as a digression, in effect prepares the way for some reintegration by the chastened self into the normal structured world. (The discourse also changes from the poetically charged birthday rhetoric to more conventional expository expression.) The practical need in a fallen world for some structure on experience is emphasized, else we are the victims of mindless and impermanent sensation:

There is hardly any thing which shows the shortsightedness or capriciousness of the imagination more than travelling does. With change of place we change our ideas; nay, our opinions and feelings. . . . We cannot enlarge our conceptions; we only shift our point of view.

The next (and final) paragraph of the essay cites journeys on which a conventionally structured relationship is desirable, indeed mandatory, as in visits to ruins, aqueducts, and pictures: "They are intelligible matters, and will bear talking about." Similarly, foreign travel requires the reassurance provided by a traveling companion of one's own nation and tongue: "In such situations, so opposite to all one's ordinary train of ideas, one seems a species by one's-self, a limb torn off from society, unless one can meet with instant fellowship and support."

This process of gradually reincorporating the self into society is briefly and nostalgically interpreted as Hazlitt remembers — quite in the spirit of his birthday experience of 1798 — a visit to France in 1802 where the ordinary limitation of foreign travel, the contact with radically different cultures, did not prevail; for then there was an "air of *general* humanity,"[17] and the *universal* language of painting in the Louvre overcame any difference of tongue. But that glorious memory must be dispatched for the sadder thought that foreign travel is ordinarily "too remote from our habitual associations to be a common topic of discourse or reference; and, like a dream or another state of existence, does not piece into our daily modes of life." Thus the essay points its conclusion to the need for the very structures it sought to escape at the start. But it should be noted that these structures are now accepted, perhaps even chosen, by the exploring self. However, even this does not provide a final resolution to the tensions of the essay: quite in the spirit of the energizing polarities he has drawn throughout, Hazlitt leaves us not with the completed exposition of a *Round Table* essay but with "contrast" and "irony," the qualities he had so admired in *The Tatler*:

> Those who wish to forget painful thoughts, do well to absent themselves for a while from the ties and objects that recall

17. My italics.

them: but we can be said only to fulfil our destiny in the place that gave us birth. I should on this account like well enough to spend the whole of my life in travelling abroad, if I could any where borrow another life to spend afterwards at home!

The various rhetorical skills we have been tracing did not desert Hazlitt at the end of his life. The long opening paragraph of "The Free Admission,"[18] published in *The New Monthly Magazine* just two months before his death, provides one of the most elaborate examples of Hazlitt's attempt to involve the reader in the expository process.

The paragraph opens with a description of the free admission as "the *lotos* of the mind," an escape from experience, "an antidote for half the ills of life." The initial movement of the paragraph is developed negatively by contrast, with a description of the disadvantages of the paid subscription. Each sentence in this initial movement is dominated by "you," the victim of the paid subscription:

If *you* have paid five guineas for a free-admission for the season, this *free-admission* turns to a mere slavery. *You* seem to have done a foolish thing, and to have committed an extravagance under the plea of economy. *You* are struck with remorse. *You* are impressed with a conviction that pleasure is not to be bought.

The movement ends with a long climactic statement of this frustrated position:

You have incurred a debt, and must go every night to redeem it; and as *you* do not like being tied to the oar, or making a toil of a pleasure, *you* stay away altogether; give up the promised luxury as a bad speculation; sit sullenly at home, or bend your loitering feet in any other direction; and putting up with the first loss, resolve never to be guilty of the like folly again.[19]

18. *Works of Hazlitt*, vol. 17, 365–70.
19. The italicized pronouns here and in my next three paragraphs are my own.

The second movement of the paragraph presents a description of the other side of the contrast, the "pure pleasure" of the holder of the free admission, and is dominated by "he." It makes its point with a mixture of positive and negative statements —

> *His* is a pure pleasure, a clear gain. *He* feels none of these irksome qualms and misgivings. *He* marches to the theatre like a favoured lover; if *he* is compelled to absent himself, he feels all the impatience and compunction of a prisoner.

— and builds to a restatement of the original "lotos" premise of the paragraph: "*he* receives a passport that is a release from care, thought, toil, for the evening, and wafts *him* into the regions of the blest!" A few lines later, human life has become for him merely "a gaudy shadow." Finally, the holder of the free admission "forgets every thing else. Why not? It is the chief and enviable transfer of *his* being from the real to the unreal world, and the changing half *his* life into a dream."

This climactic statement ends the role of the "he" that has dominated the essay in this movement. Hazlitt the "I" intensifies the point by his own experiences in the next movement, which proceeds from negative statement (awareness of the world that would limit our escape) to positive statement (total escape), which is the persistent pattern of the entire paragraph in its separate parts:

> If *I* have business that would detain me from this, *I* put it off till the morrow; if *I* have friends that call in just at the moment, let them go away under pain of bearing *my* maledictions with them. . . . But let *me* once reach, and fairly establish *myself* in this favourite seat, and *I* can bid a gay defiance to mischance, and leave debts and duns, friends and foes, objections and arguments, far behind *me*.

The "I" then achieves "a palace of delight," enjoys "golden thoughts" and "golden visions"; "the mind is full without an effort, pleased without asking why." The perfect lotos condition, beyond restriction, limitation, calculation, and worry, has been attained.

Without pause, the paragraph moves to a new consideration, "to show how much sympathy has to do with the effect"
just described. This movement is dominated by "we." The paragraph thus far has moved from the unfortunate "you" to the
happy "he" to the ecstatic "I," and part of that ecstasy was "an
atmosphere of joy" derived from the shared pleasure of others.
Again, the movement in this new section is from negative to
positive. It begins,

> let *us* suppose any one to have a free admission to the rehear-
> sals of a morning, what mortal would make use of it? One
> might as well be at the bottom of a well, or at the top of
> St. Paul's for any pleasure *we* should derive from the finest
> tragedy or comedy. . . . But reverse this cold and comfortless
> picture,

and Hazlitt embarks on an elaborate statement of the shared
joy. What becomes clear within a couple of sentences is that,
where before the theater of the free admission was an escape
from the ills of life and an entrance into a dream, it is now an
occasion for the reaffirmation of "the social principle . . . called
forth with such strength and harmony," a means of reestablish-
ing on a more generous basis the fundamental commitment to
human life and society.

Yet another movement now becomes apparent: "Nor is the
air of a playhouse favourable only to social feeling — it aids the
indulgence of solitary musing." The free admission precipitates
a rediscovery within ourselves of our happiest recollections and
most sustaining pleasures, the innocence of childhood and pictures of the age of chivalry, now rendered the more touching
with the sober awareness that those worlds have passed forever.
This bittersweet perception leads to the final climax of the paragraph. Through a series of excited, eager questions and excla-
mations "we" project ourselves, as though for compensation,
into the anticipated joys of future theatergoers, only to realize
that such joys we shall never share and that those future theatergoers must reproduce the process of our disenchantment; that,

in fact, each performance allowed by the free admission teaches the sober truth of the disenchanting limits of life:

> Who will be the Mrs. Siddons of a distant age? What future Kean shall "strut and fret his hour upon the stage," full of genius and free of errors? What favourite actor or actress will be taking their farewell benefit a hundred years hence? What plays and what players will then amuse the town? Oh, many-coloured scenes of human life! where are ye more truly represented than in the mirror of the stage? or where is that eternal principle of vicissitude which rules over ye, the painted pageant and the sudden gloom, more strikingly exemplified than here? At the entrance of our great theatres, in large capitals over the front of the stage, might be written MUTABILITY! Does not the curtain that falls each night on the pomps and vanities it was withdrawn awhile to reveal (and the next moment all is dark) afford a fine moral lesson?

A long final sentence completes the movement of the paragraph, from the theater of the free admission as an escape from the ills of life, to a perception of the theater as the truest record of human experience:

> Here, in small room, is crowded the map of human life . . . here is a glass set up clear and large enough to show us our own features and those of all mankind — here in this enchanted mirror, are represented, not darkly, but in vivid hues and bold relief, the struggle of Life and Death, the momentary pause between the cradle and the grave, with charming hopes and fears, terror and pity in a thousand modes, strange and ghastly apparitions, the events of history, the fictions of poetry (warm from the heart); all these, and more than can be numbered in my feeble page, fill that airy space where the green curtain rises, and haunt it with evanescent shapes and indescribable yearnings.

The theater now serves to offer us a comprehensive perception of the whole of life, its joys *and* sorrows, hopes *and* fears: not a separation of these mighty opposites as at the start of the paragraph, but rather their union made the more intense and dear under the shadow of mortality; not a separation of the individual from life, but "our" perception of "our" place in the unfolding pattern of the experience of all men; a journey of ourselves to the destiny of all men, passing finally beyond words to "indescribable yearnings."

Hazlitt frequently declared his pride in the continuity of his principles, opinions, and tastes. The perception of the theater found in "The Free Admission" is similar to that in the essay "On Actors and Acting" of 1817. But how much deeper and more impassioned is that perception of 1830, and how much more mature and elaborate and masterful is the art that renders that perception.

※　　※　　※

Throughout his varied career as a writer, Hazlitt sought to turn the exposition of ideas into an affective experience for the reader. As a reviewer of 1821 noted,

> By a talent almost peculiar to himself, he can connect every thing, however abstracted, with something of reality; with something that appeals at once to individual feelings and experience, and comes directly home to the business and bosoms of men.[20]

Such a praise is coordinate with Hazlitt's own expressed views on the power of language:

> Words are the signs which point out and define the objects of the highest import to the human mind. . . . The thought or impression of the moment is one thing, and it may be more or less delightful; but beyond this, it may relate to the fate or events of a whole life, and it is this moral and intellectual perspective that words convey in its full signification and extent. . . . Words are a key to the affections. They not only excite feelings, but they point to the *why* and *wherefore*.

20. *Gold's London Magazine* (June 1821), quoted in John O. Hayden, *The Romantic Reviewers 1802–1824*, p. 210.

Causes march before them, and consequences follow after them. They are links in the chain of the universe, and the grappling-irons that bind us to it.[21]

Hazlitt's domesticating of intellectual discourse by involving the reader in the experience of that discourse was symptomatic of the venture of romantic prose and one of its significant manifestations.

---

21. *Works of Hazlitt*, vol. 12, 336–37.

4. "PARTICIPATING THE TRUTHS"
IN WORDSWORTH'S PROSE

"I have not been much used to composition of any kind particularly in prose," Wordsworth wrote to his friend William Matthews in 1794; "my style therefore may frequently want fluency and sometimes perhaps perspicuity."[1] Nearly forty years later he similarly discounted his prose talent: "I am no ready master of prose writing," he declared in 1831, "having been little practised in the art."[2] Despite the disclaimers, between the time these two letters were penned, Wordsworth wrote and had published a substantial quantity of important prose — which fills three closely printed volumes in the Owen-Smyser edition of 1974 — on a range of subjects, in a variety of forms, and employing a variety of styles. There are the famous prefaces to his poetry, which range from the simply expository to the highly rhetorical and forensic; there is a commercially successful travel book, written in an appropriately simple style; there is a book-length address, of Burkean stylistic elaboration and intensity of tone, to the British people and government on political matters; there is the "Reply to 'Mathetes'" on the moral development and education of youth; there are additional treatments of literary theory and practical criticism covering the genres of epitaph and biography; and there are assorted political papers and addresses. To suggest something of the range of Wordsworth's abilities as a prose writer, I would note that works as different in subject-matter and style as the *Convention of Cintra*, the *Guide to the Lakes*, the "Reply to 'Mathetes,'" and the "Essays on Epitaphs," were all written in the same two-year period.

1. *The Letters of William and Dorothy Wordsworth: The Early Years 1787–1805*, ed. Ernest de Selincourt, rev. Mary Moorman, p. 127.

2. *The Letters of William and Dorothy Wordsworth: The Later Years*, ed. Ernest de Selincourt, p. 591.

I shall examine those texts in which Wordsworth's focus is most specifically on eliciting a "correspondent energy," "a co-operating *power*," from the reader. Wordsworth was notorious for attempting to reduce the separation between prose and poetry. One of his requirements for the success of original poems, the exertion of power or passion by the reader in reading the work, was equally true for the success of prose. A number of his own prose compositions were specifically shaped to tap this "corresponding energy" as much as to instruct in literary theory, political action, or landscape observation.

The "Preface to *Lyrical Ballads*" is as much an elaborate manipulation of the reader as Lamb's "South-Sea House"; certainly it is more a rhetorical work than the "systematic" exposition of literary theory most readers have demanded it be for nearly two centuries. The *Convention of Cintra*, Wordsworth's most ambitious prose composition, is an attempt to re-create the "sublime and pathetic emotions" of the reader more than it is an analysis of the events of the Peninsular War. Even the *Guide to the Lakes* is specifically set apart from other topographical literature by its attempt not simply to describe the surfaces of Lake Country landscapes but in addition to affect the reader's relationship to those landscapes.[3] "Essays upon Epitaphs" seek to bring the reader "into still closer communion with those primary sensations of the human heart" that are the origin of the sincere and successful examples of the genre; the reader is not

3. Previous accounts of the Lakes, such as William Gilpin's *Observations* of 1786, had largely been directed to the *eye* of the reader and had offered pictures of the surfaces of Westmorland and Cumberland mountains, valleys, and lakes. Wordsworth's emphasis was different:

In preparing this Manual, it was the Author's principal wish to furnish a Guide or Companion for the *Minds* of Persons of taste, and feeling for Landscape, who might be inclined to explore the District of the Lakes with that degree of attention to which its beauty may fairly lay claim. (*The Prose Works of William Wordsworth*, ed. W. J. B. Owen and Jane Worthington Smyser, vol. 2, 155).

For further discussion of the background and the argument of the *Guide*, see my essay "Wordsworth's *Guide to the Lakes* and the Picturesque Tradition," *Modern Philology* 61 (1964), 288–97.

simply told of certain "truths," he is asked to "participate the truths" upon which the form depends.

In short, Wordsworth's focus in some of his most creative prose is on significantly challenging and making self-conscious the reader's disposition toward his experience, whether literary, political, or topographical. His declaration of 1810 that "the excellence of writing, whether in prose or verse, consists in a conjunction of Reason and Passion,"[4] is abundantly demonstrated in his own prose, which seeks just such a totality of response.

❖   ❖   ❖

What kind of prose document is the "Preface to *Lyrical Ballads*"? What purposes control its exposition and argumentation? These questions are still appropriate because Coleridge's early charge that much of the "Preface" was "obscure beyond any necessity" continues to be echoed.[5] Each extended modern discussion represents, in James Scoggins' words, yet another "search for an underlying principle that would unite the various topics raised in it."[6] The frustrating difficulty of this search and

4. *Prose Works of Wordsworth*, vol. 2, 85.

5. Letter of 29 July 1802 to Robert Southey. *The Collected Letters of Samuel Taylor Coleridge*, ed. Earl Leslie Griggs, vol. 2, 830. Typical modern comments include: the "Preface" is "little more than a somewhat unwilling and frankly inadequate attempt" to explain the poems of the first edition (Margaret L. Barstow Greenbie, *Wordsworth's Theory of Poetic Diction* [New Haven: Yale University Press, 1917], p. xii); "Wordsworth is not an ideal expositor. . . . The argument of the Preface to *Lyrical Ballads* is not pellucid" (M. H. Abrams, *The Mirror and the Lamp*, p. 106); "none of Wordsworth's critics has succeeded in producing a logical summary of the complete text" (J. W. B. Owen, *Wordsworth's Preface to "Lyrical Ballads,"* Anglistica, vol. 9 [1957], 108); and James A. W. Heffernan (*Wordsworth's Theory of Poetry: the Transforming Imagination*) speaks of the "tortuous divagations of Wordsworth's argument in the Preface" (p. 36) and of its "disunity" (p. 47). One of the shrewdest comments I have found comes from Michael H. Friedman, who in discussing the prose of Wordsworth's later *Convention of Cintra* declares that it lacks "the semblance of clarity and simplicity that leads the unwary reader of Wordsworth's Preface to the *Lyrical Ballads* to premature certitude" (*The Making of a Tory Humanist*, p. 247).

6. "The Preface to *Lyrical Ballads*: A Revolution in Dispute," *Studies in Criticism and Aesthetics, 1600–1800*, ed. Howard Anderson and John S. Shea, p. 381. Among the attempts, Scoggins notes Stephen Parrish's underlying

the divergent "underlying principles" that continue to be turned up testify unhappily to the truth of Wordsworth's frank declaration, both at the start of the "Preface" and again near its end, that the "Preface" is *not* "a systematic defence of the theory upon which the poems were written."[7] Instead, we are told, it was meant only as a "few words of introduction" to the poems. But what intention, if any, constitutes the integrity of these more informal "words of introduction"?

An answer is provided in the fifth paragraph, with the following three-stage argument:

(1) "It is supposed, that by the act of writing in verse an Author makes a formal engagement that he will gratify certain known habits of association; that he not only thus apprizes the Reader that certain classes of ideas and expressions will be found in his book, but that others will be carefully excluded."

(2) The poems of *Lyrical Ballads* vary widely from current practice and may create for the reader "feelings of strangeness and aukwardness."

(3) "I hope therefore the Reader will not censure me, if I attempt to state what I have proposed to myself to perform; and also, (as far as the limits of a preface will permit) to explain some of the chief reasons which have determined me in the choice of my purpose: that at least he may be spared any unpleasant feeling of disappointment, and that I myself may be protected from the most dishonorable accusation which can be brought against an Author, namely, that of an indolence which prevents him from endeavouring to ascertain

principle as Wordsworth's "concern with psychological truth and dramatic method," and Owen's description of its "comprehensive motive in a definition of a permanent rhetoric." Scoggins himself offers the underlying principle as Wordsworth's desire to "provide a new *kind* of pleasure" (p. 383).

7. "Preface to *Lyrical Ballads, with Pastoral and Other Poems*" (1802), in *Literary Criticism of William Wordsworth*, ed. Paul M. Zall, pp. 39, 57. All quotations are from the 1802 version of the "Preface" as reproduced in Zall and will be cited hereafter in my text by page number.

what is his duty, or, when his duty is ascertained, prevents him from performing it." (pp. 39–40)

Thus, the goal of the "Preface" is *the creation of a mutually understanding and beneficial relationship between reader and writer.* The means to that goal is such exposition as will establish the *credibility of the writer* in his choice of poetic intentions. As Wordsworth states at another point, "What I wished *chiefly* to attempt, at present, was to justify myself for having written under the impression of [certain critical beliefs]" (p. 56). Instead of constituting a "systematic defence" whose purpose would be the demonstrable truth of the propositions advanced, the "introductory remarks" are rhetorical and apologetic, seeking at best probability or "presumption" about the truths of the propositions. Wordsworth makes this clear in two significantly echoing passages that constitute a frame for the entire "Preface." The fourth paragraph opens:

> Several of my Friends are anxious for the success of these Poems from a belief, that, if the views with which they were composed were indeed realized, *a class of Poetry would be produced, well adapted to interest mankind permanently, and not unimportant in the multiplicity, and in the quality of its moral relations*: and on this account they have advised me to prefix a systematic defense of the theory upon which the poems were written. (p. 39, my italics)

The penultimate paragraph of the "Preface" concludes:

> *it has been less my present aim to prove*, that the interest excited by some other kinds of poetry is less vivid, and less worthy of the nobler powers of the mind, *than to offer reasons for presuming*, that, if the object which I have proposed to myself were adequately attained, *a species of poetry would be produced, which is genuine poetry; in its nature well adapted to interest mankind permanently, and likewise important in the multiplicity and quality of its moral relations*. (p. 62, my italics)

Though frequently overlapping in the text, a number of separate tactics can be isolated as Wordsworth's persistent means of achieving his rhetorical and apologetic goals: his constant address to, or inclusion of, the reader in the evolution of the discourse; his delineation of the character and mind of the persona; and his employment of appropriate modes of style and argument. The examination of these tactics will not remove the "logical inconsistencies" in poetic theory that have been alleged by readers of the "Preface"; rather, the examination is merely to define the nature of the document as an integral prose composition. One of the most recent ventures in removing these "inconsistencies" has been the demonstration of the essentially rhetorical nature of the poetic theory.[8] In view of this new emphasis, it would seem appropriate to note how rhetorical is the prose document in which this theory is contained and by which it is shaped.

The most obvious and superficial sign of Wordsworth's paramount concern to create and to maintain an accommodating relationship between reader and writer is the constant address to the "reader" or "we." Scarcely a paragraph passes without such an address appealing to the reader's experience, requiring his judgment, asking his indulgence, taking account of his objections, or assuming his agreement. The following, taken from diverse parts of the "Preface," are typical: "I will not abuse the indulgence of my Reader" (p. 43); "I point the Reader's attention to this" (p. 43); "I shall request the Reader's permission" (p. 44); "[This is] a canon of criticism which the Reader will conclude he must utterly reject" (p. 45); "[I appeal] to the Reader's own experience" (p. 56); "I have therefore to request, that the Reader would abide independently by his own feelings" (p. 61). Thus the reader's presence and his assumed response are always in view, as are the personality and the voice of the writer or persona of the "remarks." In these terms, the five-paragraph introduction should be seen as the traditional exordium of a rhetorical address, in which the speaker seeks to elicit

8. Gene W. Ruoff, "Wordsworth on Language: Toward a Radical Poetics for English Romanticism," *The Wordsworth Circle* 3 (1972), 204–11; Stephen M. Parrish, *The Art of the "Lyrical Ballads"* (Cambridge: Harvard University Press, 1973).

an initially favorable reaction by ethical appeal, that is, by evidence of his responsible and sympathetic character.

We learn in the first paragraph that *Lyrical Ballads* was not conceived as an arrogant gesture of originality but as an "experiment" undertaken in the hope of providing a new source of genuine poetic pleasure for the reader. The speaker's good judgment, as well as a quiet suggestion that the "experiment" has already met with some success, is indicated in the second paragraph where Wordsworth's anticipation of critical response to the poems has proved accurate, except, as he adds at the end of the paragraph, "I have pleased a greater number, than I ventured to hope I should please." In the third paragraph, we are told that a sense of his own "weakness" and a desire to afford his reader "variety" led him to include poems by Coleridge; but, he prudently adds, he would not have sought this aid if the additional poems did not have the "same tendency as my own" (pp. 38–39). Here and throughout the exordium, Wordsworth maintains a balance between his own integrity and judgment on the one hand and his concern for the pleasure and the enlightenment of his audience on the other.

The final two paragraphs of the introduction are similarly controlled by the writer's sense of responsibility toward and respect for his audience and by other evidence of his character and credibility. In addition to passages already cited, one might note the first of the explanations for rejecting a "systematic defense":

> I knew that on this occasion the Reader would look coldly
> upon my arguments, since I might be suspected of having
> been principally influenced by the selfish and foolish hope of
> *reasoning* him into an approbation of these particular Poems.

The second of the explanations is contained in a sentence of closely connected cause-and-effect clauses:

> For to treat the subject with the clearness and coherence, of
> which I believe it susceptible, it would be necessary to give a
> full account of the present state of the public taste in this

> country, and to determine how far this taste is healthy or depraved; which, again, could not be determined, without pointing out, in what manner language and the human mind act and re-act on each other, and without retracing the revolutions, not of literature alone, but likewise of society itself. (p. 39)

This represents one of the manifestations of what I shall call the "credible reasoning style" of the "Preface"; that is to say, Wordsworth employed in the "Preface" a distinctive mode of sentence structure or paragraph organization whenever he was concerned to describe or to reenact his reasoning process in place of a formal demonstration of the truth of the premises of that process. However incomplete this procedure might be in terms of "systematic defense," it is compatible with the chosen rhetorical goals of the work.

Following the exordium, the first section of the internal exposition states the "principal object" sought in the poems and then marks off two features distinguishing these poems from other "popular poems of the day." The rhetorical procedures already evident in the exordium are here in full play. However unique the "object" might be considered, "to chuse incidents or situations from common life and to relate or describe them throughout . . . in a selection of language really used by men," the "final cause" of the selected purpose encompasses the reader:

> and further, and above all, to make these incidents and situations interesting by tracing in them, truly though not ostentatiously, the primary laws of *our* nature: chiefly, as far as regards the manner in which *we* associate ideas in a state of excitement. (p. 40, my italics)

"Low and rustic life" as a source of both "incidents" and "language" is chosen in order that "our" associations of ideas might be more accurately observed and communicated. The sentence that presents this "argument" is the first example of the balanced structure of Wordsworth's "credible reasoning style" substituting for a formal demonstration. In chapter seventeen of

Biographia Literaria the logician Coleridge precisely took issue with the premises of this rhetorically and stylistically sustained argumentation:

> Low and rustic life was generally chosen, *because in that condition*, the essential passions of the heart find a better soil in which they can attain their maturity, are less under restraint, and speak a plainer and more emphatic language; *because in that condition* of life our elementary feelings co-exist in a state of greater simplicity, and, consequently, may be more accurately contemplated, and more forcibly communicated; *because* the manners of rural life germinate from those elementary feelings; and, from the necessary character of rural occupations, are more easily comprehended; and are more durable; and lastly, *because in that condition* — the passions of men are incorporated with the beautiful and permanent forms of nature. The language, too, of these men is adopted . . . *because* such men hourly communicate with the best objects from which the best parts of language are originally derived; and *because*, from their rank in society and the sameness and narrow circle of their intercourse, being less under the influence of social vanity they convey their feelings and notions in simple and unelaborated expressions. (p. 41, my italics)

In describing the first distinction of his poems from other popular verses, the presence of a "worthy purpose," Wordsworth tempers his apparent assertion of the originality and superiority of the poet — "Poems to which any value can be attached, were never produced on any variety of subjects but by a man, who being possessed of more than usual organic sensibility, had also thought long and deeply" — with a long sentence that treats as one the psychological processes of both poet and reader. In effect, the sentence attempts to turn readers into poets engaged in a rhetorical enterprise of "enlightening" and "ameliorating" an audience:

> For our continued influxes of feeling are modified and directed by our thoughts, which are indeed the representatives of all our past feelings; and, as by contemplating the relation

> of these general representatives to each other we discover what is really important to men, so, by the repetition and continuance of this act, our feelings will be connected with important subjects, till at length, if we be originally possessed of much sensibility, such habits of mind will be produced, that, by obeying blindly and mechanically the impulses of those habits, we shall describe objects, and utter sentiments, of such a nature and in such connection with each other, that the understanding of the being to whom we address ourselves, if he be in a healthful state of association, must necessarily be in some degree enlightened, and his affections ameliorated. (p. 42)

We have seen this identification of prose reader as poet already in Hazlitt and will find it again in Coleridge; it is one of the clearest manifestations of a main motive or impulse in the most original romantic prose writing on poetry.

The second distinction from the "popular poetry of the day," namely, that "the feeling therein developed gives importance to the action and situation," is similarly focused with the reader in mind:

> one being is elevated above another, in proportion as he possesses this capability. It has therefore appeared to me, that to endeavour to produce or enlarge this capability is one of the best services in which, at any period, a Writer can be engaged. (p. 43)

Using the common rhetorical topos of *a fortiori*, Wordsworth develops his point by noting the heightened value of this service at the present time: "For a multitude of causes, unknown to former times, are now acting with a combined force to blunt the discriminating powers of the mind." The apparent self-importance of his service is in turn immediately tempered by an acknowledgment of his "feeble efforts" in such a difficult task, by his corresponding reliance on certain "indestructible powers" both in the human mind and in the objects the mind encounters, and by his confidence that "men of greater powers" will counter the danger "with far more distinguished success" (p. 44). Again, Wordsworth rhetorically seeks a balance between the intended value of his services to the reader and his prudence and humility in offering and assessing that service.

The rest of the "Preface" devotes itself primarily to the material cause of language and style in poetry, with a continuing emphasis of the reader-writer relationship and the apologetic nature of the discourse. In terms of the writer, Wordsworth takes up the topic precisely "that I may not be censured for not having performed what I never intended"; and with the reader in mind, "personifications of abstractions," except when "prompted by passion," are "utterly rejected" as an "ordinary device" of style, because "I have wished to keep my Reader in the company of flesh and blood, persuaded that by so doing I shall interest him." A similar rejection of poetic diction rhetorically focuses on the writer's character, both in his endeavor to achieve truth by such a rejection ("I have endeavoured to look steadily at my subject") and in noting the difficulties this integrity causes him as poet: "it has necessarily cut me off from a large portion of phrases and figures of speech" readily used for generations to create poems (pp. 44–45).

The most revolutionary aspect of Wordsworth's argument about style is the "defense" of "prosaisms" in poetry. He is presumably confident enough of the reader's understanding of the critical principles thus far outlined that, where before the writer "utterly rejected" personifications of abstractions, the reader is now called on to "conclude he must utterly reject" the critical doctrine that ridicules "prosaisms." The "defense" is developed with two assertions: "the language of a large portion of every good poem . . . must necessarily . . . in no respect differ from that of good prose, but likewise that some of the most interesting parts of the best poems will be found to be strictly the language of prose, when prose is well written"; and "there neither is, nor can be, any essential difference between the language of prose and metrical composition." Instead of a logical proof of either position, Wordsworth employs rhetorical means, which is in the first case an illustration (Gray's sonnet) and in the second case an amplification[9] of his position. The latter invokes the heightened style of poetry with an extended personification and even the quotation of poetry. The style of this passage in fact illustrates the point about the identity of poetry and prose "when prose is well written." The rhetorical presentation in place of logical demonstration, it should be noted, is freely couched in the now assured agreement of reader and writer:

> We are fond of tracing the resemblance between Poetry and Painting, and, accordingly, we call them Sisters: but where shall we find bonds of connection sufficiently strict to typify the affinity betwixt metrical and prose composition? They both speak by and to the same organs; the bodies in which both of them are clothed may be said to be of the same substance, their affections are kindred and almost identical, not necessarily differing even in degree; Poetry sheds no tears "such as Angels weep," but natural and human tears; she can boast of no celestial Ichor that distinguishes her vital juices from those of prose; the same human blood circulates through the veins of them both. (p. 47)

From this point onward, the identity of reader and writer on all points of exposition is assumed; reader joins writer against the opponents of the critical positions outlined in the rest of the "Preface" on such topics as the nature of the poet, the end of poetry, the role of meter. I shall therefore turn to the conclusion where Wordsworth now quite appropriately engaged in a series of intimate and direct statements to the reader, statements that would have been unacceptable and counterproductive earlier. He acknowledges that his poems may have serious "defects" of association and that he may have written "upon unworthy subjects"; but he then frankly says in balance, "the Reader ought never to forget that he is himself exposed to the same errors as

9. For Wordsworth's use of rhetorical amplification here and elsewhere in the "Preface," I am indebted to Don H. Bialostosky, "Coleridge's Interpretation of Wordsworth's Preface to *Lyrical Ballads*," 919.

the Poet, and perhaps in a much greater degree." Although he urges the reader to judge by his own feelings, he requests the admission that the reader may lack the "thought and long continued intercourse with the best models of composition" to develop the taste necessary to appreciate him and other poets (pp. 59–61). James Heffernan has noted a logical contradiction between these statements, the "kind of dissonance" he finds "characteristic of the Preface."[10] These statements present a logical contradiction perhaps, but it is one consistent with the rhetorical nature of the "Preface," which throughout compliments and instructs, defers to and leads the reader.

In the penultimate paragraph, Wordsworth accepts the possibility that the reader may still feel attachment to other kinds of poetry for the different kinds of pleasure they provide. He quietly acknowledges that "there is a host of arguments in these feelings." Even more, he risks saying — what has never before been so directly stated — that to enjoy his poems means the sacrifice of other kinds of poetry.[11] He cites the limits of the "Preface" as forestalling a full debate on how the pleasure of those other kinds is produced in distinction to the "purer, more lasting, more exquisite nature" of his own. In conclusion, he reminds the reader that he has only sought to offer "reasons for presuming" that he has presented a genuinely valuable poetry; and the "Preface" ends with the writer falling back in second place to the reader, who is now asked to render judgment on the success of the entire venture of *Lyrical Ballads* and for that matter on the success of the rhetorical strategies of the "Preface" itself:

> From what has been said, and from a perusal of the Poems, the Reader will be able clearly to perceive the object which I

10. *Wordsworth's Theory of Poetry*, p. 92n.
11. George Saintsbury (*A History of Criticism and Literary Taste in Europe*, 2d ed. [New York, 1906], vol. 3, 204) sees this as a "candid but singularly damaging admission." It is not "damaging," I would argue, when the admission is viewed in terms of the changes in reader-writer relationship evolved in the course of the "Preface."

have proposed to myself; he will determine how far I have attained this object; and, what is a much more important question, whether it be worth attaining; and upon the decision of these two questions will rest my claim to the approbation of the public. (p. 62)

Given the striking claims of the "Preface" and their significance in the history of English poetic theory, it is not surprising that the document has been subjected to logical scrutiny by critics and by scholars from the time of publication to the present. Given the rhetorical nature of the document, it is not surprising that such an attempt has never completely succeeded. Many of its detractors have asked the work to be the "systematic defense" Wordsworth never wrote and have accordingly missed the integrity of the work as rhetoric and as apologia. In the "Preface," Wordsworth *as writer* was primarily concerned with *creating a favorably disposed and activated reader*; the success or the failure of the "Preface" as prose document must be considered in these terms.

❖   ❖   ❖

As I indicated earlier, the years between 1808 and 1810 were the richest in prose composition during Wordsworth's lifetime, when he produced *Convention of Cintra*, *Guide to the Lakes*, "Reply to 'Mathetes,'" and "Essays upon Epitaphs." These works directly overlap in time with the genesis, composition, and publication of Coleridge's *The Friend* (1 June 1809 to 15 March 1810), for which Wordsworth specifically composed the "Reply" and in which the first of the "Essays upon Epitaphs" appeared. The connections between *The Friend* and *Cintra* are particularly close and intriguing. Coleridge was living with the Wordsworths at Grasmere in the fall of 1808 planning *The Friend*, a major prose work that had as its subject "PRINCIPLES . . . their subordination, their connection, and their application, in all the divisions of our duties and of our pleasures."[12] At the

12. *The Friend*, ed. Barbara E. Rooke, in *The Collected Works of Samuel Taylor Coleridge*, vol. 4, ii, 30.

very same time Wordsworth began *his* major prose work, in its original title *The Convention of Cintra brought to the Test of Principles*.[13] In *The Friend* Coleridge acknowledged an identical impulse behind his work and Wordsworth's when he hailed the author of *Cintra* as "a fellow-labourer in the same vineyard, actuated by the same motives and teaching the same principles."[14]

Certainly the two works had similar intentions with regard to the reader. "I wished to convey not instruction merely," Coleridge wrote, "but fundamental instruction; not so much to shew my Reader this or that Fact, as to kindle his own Torch for him, and leave it to himself to chuse the particular objects, which he might wish to examine by it's light." Such a purpose required of the reader not only "ATTENTION generally" but also "THOUGHT sometimes," the latter being defined as "the voluntary production in our own minds of those states of consciousness, to which, as to his fundamental facts, the Writer has referred us."[15] These remarks are glosses on all of Wordsworth's efforts in the prose of the period, but most especially on *Convention of Cintra*, which seeks a radical reader involvement far in excess of even the persistent strategies of the "Preface."

13. *The Letters of William and Dorothy Wordsworth: The Middle Years Part I 1806–1811*, ed. Ernest de Selincourt, rev. Mary Moorman, p. 278.

14. *The Friend*, ii, 108. There are numerous correspondences, in some cases, identities, in subject matter and sentiment between the two works. The following are typical: defense against a charge of "presumption" in criticizing political and philosophical opponents (*The Friend*, ii, 32–36; *Prose Works of Wordsworth*, vol. 1, 303), the disproportion of human passions to worldly objects capable of satisfying them (*The Friend*, ii, 31; *Prose Works of Wordsworth*, vol. 1, 339), the observation that men are better than their principles, whereas before principles were better than men (*The Friend*, ii, 28; *Prose Works of Wordsworth*, vol. 1, 317), similar treatments of Napoleon (*The Friend*, ii, 83–84; *Prose Works of Wordsworth*, vol. 1, 312–13), "curiosity" rather than self-reflection and useful knowledge as the motive of modern readers and writers (*The Friend*, ii, 151, 217–18, 273, 276, 286; *Prose Works of Wordsworth*, vol. 1, 230). See also footnote 17.

Coleridge apparently took a direct hand in the composition of *Cintra* at one point; he claimed to have written much of that segment that was published in *The Courier*, 13 January 1809 (*Collected Letters of Coleridge*, vol. 3, 164.

15. *The Friend*, ii, 276–77.

> . . . through the human heart [I] explore my way;
> And look and listen — gathering, where I may,
> Triumph, and thought no bondage can restrain.
>   — Sonnet "Composed while the Author was En-
>   gaged in writing a Tract occasioned by the Conven-
>   tion of Cintra"

"THE CONVENTION, recently concluded by the Generals at the head of the British army in Portugal, is one of the most important events of our time"[16] — Wordsworth opens his longest, most anxiously composed and rhetorically most ambitious work with a sentence markedly simple in its construction and in its apparent meaning. The simplicity of construction is, in fact, atypical: the entire text is dominated by the long, frequently periodic, and always highly wrought sentence, in which a weight of conditions, qualifications, and perspectives is brought to bear on a declarative statement or conclusion. The reader, if he is to understand the work at all, cannot avoid a persistent participation in the strenuous activity of style. In addition, the "importance" of the event is far from being apparent, that several paragraphs later Wordsworth lists as one of the aims of his treatise to make clear "wherein the real importance of the event lies." To accomplish this, he must shift attention away from the expected

16. The historical background for the *Convention* is briefly as follows. In the fall of 1807, French military forces entered Spain in order to conquer Britain's traditional ally, Portugal. Under the pretext of supporting the army in Portugal, more French troops subsequently occupied Spain, forcing the monarchy of Charles IV and his son Ferdinand to abdicate (May 1808) and placing Napoleon's brother Joseph on the throne. Spanish cities rose in spontaneous revolt. On 1 August, British forces landed in Portugal and defeated the forces of the French General Junot. On 30 August, the "Convention" (treaty) of Cintra was negotiated, presumably to formalize the French defeat. To the consternation of the British public, General Junot was granted the most lenient terms of surrender, including transportation of the defeated troops back to France with all the plunder of their Portuguese conquest. As part of a widespread movement of protest and petition in England against the government's support of the Convention, Wordsworth (with others) attempted to organize a county meeting, which was met with opposition from the local political power Lord Lonsdale; in the words of Southey, Wordsworth then "went home to ease his heart by writing a pamphlet."

details of warfare and armistice papers to the *internal life — the passions and moral sensibilities — of the reader*, who is even more the center of concern here, and certainly at a far deeper level, than in the "Preface to *Lyrical Ballads*." The change from the relatively uninvolved style and the relatively traditional rhetorical strategies of the "Preface" to verbal complexity and the subtle maneuverings among the reader's deepest confidences and fears says much for the range and the ambition of Wordsworth's exploration of the province of prose.

The rhetorical focus of the work is initiated in the first paragraph. The impersonal opening sentence is followed by a shift in the second sentence to "what this nation has felt and still feels upon the subject. . . ." In the succeeding two sentences these feelings receive greater definition and presence until the paragraph reaches its climax in the penultimate sentence with its epistrophic construction and its final accent on the key word of feeling, "betrayed":

There have been four extended discussions and two separate editions of *The Convention of Cintra* in the twentieth century. A. V. Dicey's edition (London: Humphrey Milford, 1915) was followed by his *The Statesmanship of Wordsworth An Essay* (Oxford: Clarendon Press, 1917), which extracted and discussed five major themes or "doctrines" in the treatise but did not deal specifically with the organization or rhetoric of the work; George Kent Thomas's *Wordsworth's Dirge and Promise: Napoleon, Wellington, and the Convention of Cintra* (Lincoln: University of Nebraska Press, 1971) is concerned with the historical context, the process of composition, and the "Doctrine of National Happiness" (Professor Thomas has also written the short introduction to a facsimile edition of *Cintra*, published by Brigham Young University Press, 1983); Friedman's *Tory Humanist* does subject the work to a "close reading" (p. 247), but Friedman's frankly ideological approach (Freudian and Marxian) causes him to ignore even the most obvious of Wordsworth's specific divisions of the argument as argument, much less the more sophisticated rhetorical procedures. The most valuable treatment to date of the art of *Cintra* is found in David R. Sanderson's "Wordsworth's World, 1809: A Stylistic Study of the Cintra Pamphlet," 104–13. Sanderson has valuable things to say throughout about the function of style, but he does not deal with the organization or the larger rhetorical configurations of the work.

All my quotations from *Cintra* are from the text in the first volume of *Prose Works of Wordsworth*, and will be cited hereafter by page number.

> Yet was the event by none received as an open and measurable affliction: It had indeed features bold and intelligible to everyone; but there was an under-expression which was strange, dark, and mysterious — and, accordingly as different notions prevailed, or the object was looked at in different points of view, we were astonished like men who are overwhelmed without forewarning — fearful like men who feel themselves to be helpless, and indignant and angry like men who are betrayed. (p. 224)

The text proceeds with a repeated movement, which extends over four paragraphs, of making even more present to the reader the keenness of the emotional "earthquake" created by the Convention in its betrayal of moral sensibility; for it is in this violation of the *reader's* sensibility and of his unqualified confidence in the triumph of a just cause that a true perspective for judging the event and for understanding its "importance" will be found. The second paragraph recalls the year 1808, specifically the strong personal involvement and the "force of *inspiration* felt by the British public toward their army in support of the Spanish cause. Indeed, before Wordsworth mentions almost as an afterthought the strength of the military forces going to assist the peninsular revolt, we are extensively told of the British soldier's *affective* disposition and the humane ties created by the situation:

> If the conduct of the rapacious and merciless adversary rendered it neither easy nor wise — made it, I might say, impossible to give way to that unqualified admiration of courage and skill, made it impossible in relation to him to be exalted by those triumphs of the courteous affections, and to be purified by those refinements of civility which do, more than any thing, reconcile a man of thoughtful mind and humane dispositions to the horrors of ordinary war; it was felt that for such loss the benign and accomplished soldier would upon this mission be abundantly recompensed by the enthusiasm of fraternal love with which his Ally, the oppressed people whom he was going to aid in rescuing themselves, would re-

ceive him; and that this, and the virtues which he would witness in them, would furnish his heart with never-failing and
far nobler objects of complacency and admiration.

The force of these feelings added to the military discipline of
the army completes the extended development of the paragraph
in recovering the exhilaration and noble hopes of the experience of 1808 — only to have these fall in the deliberately under-
stated conclusion:

> The army proved its prowess in the field; and what has been
> the result is attested, and long will be attested, by the down-
> cast looks — the silence — the passionate exclamations — the
> sighs and shame of every man who is worthy to breathe the
> air or to look upon the green- fields of Liberty in this blessed
> and highly-favoured Island which we inhabit. (pp. 225–26)

The third and fourth paragraphs repeat and intensify this
pattern by adopting a larger temporal frame for its drama of
hope and betrayal and by focusing exclusively on the citizen-
reader. This reader's feelings are reviewed from the start of
hostilities with France in 1793, when many conscientiously op-
posed the conflict; until 1802, when the "selfish tyranny and
lawless ambition" of Napoleon caused the war to be embraced
by many, but in a somewhat grim and necessitated spirit; and,
finally, to 1808 and the instantaneous admiration and abundant
hope provided for that embrace by the peninsular uprising. The
frame expands to include the equally enthusiastic and hopeful
feelings of the Spaniards toward the British, as each nation cast
aside age-old suspicions and religious and political differences.
The hope provided by the purity and totality of commitment on
both sides is again undercut; the understatement of the results
of the Convention frustrates the elaborate rhetorical development that has immediately preceded:

> To assist them and their neighbours the Portuguese in the at-
> tainment of this end, we sent to them in love and in friendship
> a powerful army to aid — to invigorate — and to chastise: —

they landed; and the first proof they afforded of their being worthy to be sent on such a service — the first pledge of amity given by them was the victory of Vimiera; the second pledge (and this was from the hand of their Generals,) was the Convention of Cintra. (pp. 226–29)

These initial five paragraphs constitute the first segment of *Cintra* and were in fact published as a single installment in the *Courier* of 27 December 1808. Their repeated movement of richly and multiply derived hope followed by abrupt betrayal provides the basic metaphor for the long work and determines both the rhetorical procedures and the thematic development. Wordsworth will attempt to reverse the debilitating pattern by offering practical political and military advice but more significantly *by reviving in the reader* the original passionate response of hope and conviction of justice.

In paragraph six, Wordsworth begins the work of reconstruction. He announces formally his intention of recalling "those words and facts, which first carried the conviction [of the righteousness of the Spanish cause] to our hearts: that, as far as it is possible, we may see as we then saw, and feel as we then felt." But because this review may only intensify the sense of betrayal, Wordsworth first offers some immediate grounds of hope: the Spanish military force now recognizes that success lies in a guerrilla war; there is now a trusted government to lead them; and all Spaniards "ought to be encouraged to deem themselves an army." However, these short-term grounds of hope involve a larger issue embodied in the last of the three; even beyond a universal military spirit, the Spanish people must recognize that "in the moral virtues and qualities of passion which belong to a people, must the ultimate salvation of a people be sought for. . . . They must now be taught, that their strength *chiefly* lies in moral qualities" (pp. 230–35). The same trust in sensibility that Wordsworth seeks to create in his betrayed British reader he also seeks to create in the Spaniards.

Having announced and already partially illustrated his rhetorical means, the revivification of feeling, Wordsworth defines the goal or "main object" of his treatise:

to assist some portion of my readers to form an estimate of the grounds of hope and fear in the present effort of liberty against oppression, in the present or any future struggle which justice will have to maintain against might. (p. 237)

The examination of the limited event of the Convention is supportive and illustrative of this goal; the prerequisite for the examination of the Convention is the creation of the perspective of hope lodged in humane dispositions and in the passion for justice versus selfishness and tyranny. One source of this necessary perspective has already been provided by a review of the "feelings of the people and of Spain towards each other"; a second source for this perspective is provided now by reviewing "by what barrier of aversion, scarcely less sacred, the people of the *Peninsula* were divided from their enemies, — their feelings towards them, and their hopes for themselves" (p. 237). The succeeding ten paragraphs are devoted to this source.

Wordsworth first presents the brutalities of the French military operations against the Spanish and Portuguese and the insulting and hypocritical statements of French "concern" for these countries, amounting to a most "searching warfare against the conscience and the reason" (p. 242). But balancing and outweighing these outrages are the "consolations, resolves, and hopes" of the struggling nations: first is the Spanish recognition of these attacks as divine arousals from "the state of lethargy in which we [the Spanish] indulged, and to make us acquainted with our rights, our glory, and the inviolable duty which we owe to our holy religion and our monarch" (p. 243); second is that the calamities call up the "solace" of "the illustrious deeds of their ancestors" and with it "the highest obligations of duty to their posterity" (p. 244); finally, the Spanish have "bolder hopes rising from a confidence in the supremacy of justice" (p. 245). In short, in their response the Spanish convert the polarities of the treatise from betrayal to hope.

The extent to which all of Wordsworth's efforts thus far exist for the reader's response is made clear in the direct statement:

> *I will now beg of my reader to pause a moment, and to review in his*
> *own mind the whole of what has been laid before him.* . . . It is not
> from any thought that I am communicating new information,
> that I have dwelt thus long upon this subject, but *to recall to*
> *the reader his own knowledge, and to re-infuse into that knowledge a*
> *breath and life of appropriate feeling; because the bare sense of*
> *wisdom is nothing without its powers, and it is only in these feelings*
> *that the powers of wisdom exist.* (pp. 247–48, my italics) [17]

With this highly personalized perspective now established for
both sides, the sense of enthusiasm and righteousness derived
from deep-seated confidence in the triumph of a just cause,
Wordsworth turns to the examination of the Convention itself.

The examination falls into two lengthy divisions that are
clearly marked in a text not otherwise notable for its overt signs
of organization. Twelve paragraphs are devoted to the "military
results" of the treaty (pp. 249–64), twelve to its "political in-
justice and moral depravity" (pp. 265–77). Wordsworth maintains the previous perspective by presenting many of the historic details in terms of their reception by the British public,
and in so doing he repeats the now clearly established pattern
of hopes betrayed. He further maintains the perspective by
directly applying the principles of moral sensibility to the
behavior of the British authorities in Portugal: for example,
Wellesley's denomination of the French general Junot under his
presumptuously adopted Portuguese title "affords too strong a
suspicion of a deadness to the moral interests of the cause in
which [Wellesley] was engaged" (p. 251); or later, "the Span-
iard could not *ultimately* be benefited but by allies acting under
the same impulses of honour, rouzed by a sense of their wrongs,
and sharing their loves and hatreds — above all, their *passion* for
justice" (p. 262).

17. Cf. Coleridge's similar statement in *The Friend* that his purpose is not
to describe the "new" but "to support all old and venerable Truths; and by
them to support, to kindle, to project the Spirit; to make the Reason spread
Light over the Feelings, to make our Feelings, with their vital warmth, actu-
alize our Reason" (ii, 73).

The central focus of *Cintra* on the internal drama of moral sensibility and passion and its pattern of hope and betrayal are nowhere clearer than in the paragraphs following on the two sections devoted to the Convention documents. The reader's attention is first directed to the dismaying effects of the Convention on the people of Portugal: the "shock to their confidence in themselves" and more seriously their doubts about the value of independence and liberty for which they had been struggling (p. 280). Next, the experience of the Portuguese vis-à-vis the British people is shown to have been duplicated in the tandem experience of the British people vis-à-vis their government when the news of the Convention was first revealed; from their noble commitment to the independence of their suffering allies, they were forced back to a defense of the most elementary prerequisite for their own liberty, the right to petition (p. 281–84).

Wordsworth's defense of the right to petition "in this or any case" reposes on the basic premise of passionate sensibility in the search for justice and as a guide to political action:

> But in all that regarded the destinies of Spain, and her own as connected with them, the voice of Britain had the unquestionable sound of inspiration. If the gentle passions of pity, love, and gratitude, be porches of the temple; if the sentiments of admiration and rivalry be pillars upon which the structure is sustained; if, lastly, hatred, and anger, and vengeance, be steps which, by a mystery of nature, lead to the House of Sanctity: — then was it manifest to what power the edifice was consecrated; and that the voice within was of Holiness and Truth. (p. 290)

This virtual canonization of internal feelings burst through the surface of *Cintra* at almost the exact center of the work; everything else anticipates or follows from this. Seventeen paragraphs richer in style and stronger and more urgent in tone than anything before or after are devoted to a direct and impassioned presentation of these feelings as the tone of the text is elevated through the use of biblical echoes and cadences. The following excerpts are typical:

There is no middle course: two masters cannot be served: — Justice must either be enthroned above might, and the moral law take place of the edicts of selfish passion; or the heart of the people, which alone can sustain the efforts of the people, will languish: their desires will not spread beyond the plough and the loom, the field and the fireside: the sword will appear to them an emblem of no promise; an instrument of no hope; an object of indifference, of disgust, or fear. (p. 292)

Let the fire, which is never wholly to be extinguished, break out afresh; let but the human creature be rouzed; whether he have lain heedless and torpid in religious or civil slavery — have languished under a thraldom, domestic or foreign, or under both these alternately — or have drifted about a helpless member of a clan of disjointed and feeble barbarians; let him rise and act; — and his domineering imagination, by which from childhood he has been betrayed, and the debasing affections, which it has imposed upon him, will from that moment participate the dignity of the newly ennobled being whom they will now acknowledge for their master; and will further him in his progress, whatever be the object at which he aims. (p. 294)

With this, Wordsworth turns to the final section of the treatise, the means of reparation for the errors of the Convention. These means are based on the principles exposed throughout the work but most forcefully in the preceding section. The first and most extensively developed of these is "a knowledge of human nature directing the operations of our government" rather than an exclusive reliance on physical force and short-term advantage.

It surely then behoves those who are in authority — to look to the state of their own minds . . . that the People might see, upon great occasions, — in the practice of its Rulers — a more adequate reflection of its own wisdom and virtue. (p. 310)

In terms of the inward emphasis of *Cintra*, this precept is appropriately placed first; in effect, the rulers are asked to adopt the same reflective activity to which the reader has been called throughout the work. Two other means of more material nature are then considered: either sending a large force into the peninsula, or at least sending armaments and other military supplies in large quantity.

The consistency of the principles of *Cintra* is clearly illustrated in Wordsworth's handling of the objection to sending troops, an objection drawn from the imagined invincibility of Napoleon, who is the Satanic figure of the work precisely because his power consists in the utter rejection of those passions of justice and the humane affections in which Wordsworth has been placing his trust. But the source of Napoleon's strength is, in fact, the testimony to his weakness. Not being based on a passion for justice, his power has in it "nothing *inherent* and *permanent*." Wordsworth continues, "Two signal overthrows in pitched battles would, I believe, go far to destroy it" (p. 313). It should be noted that Wordsworth's "proof" for this position lies only in the psychological and moral assumptions he has used persistently throughout the work, not in historical analysis or in formal argument.

Against the lack of principle shown by British politicians in failing to counter Napoleon's "strength" by their support of the Convention, Wordsworth moves within the rhetorical structure once again to hope in the determination and the enthusiasm of the Spanish people for national independence. Even if the material state of Spain might be improved by submission to Napoleon in terms of the end of feudal abuses and the achievement of "certain insignificant privileges" (p. 323), the loss of independence would be a disastrous price:

> Not by bread alone is the life of Man sustained; not by raiment alone is he warmed; — but by the genial and vernal inmate of the breast, which at once pushes forth and cherishes; by self-support and self-sufficing endeavours; by anticipations, apprehensions, and active remembrances; by elasticity under insult, and firm resistance to injury; by joy, and by love; by pride which his imagination gathers in from afar; by patience, because life wants not promises; by admiration;

by gratitude which — debasing him not when his fellow-being is its object — habitually expands itself, for his elevation, in complacency towards his Creator.

Now, to the existence of these blessings, national independence is indispensible; and many of them it will itself produce and maintain. (pp. 326–27)

Then follows a series of directives to the leaders of Spain to adopt the same principles he has urged on the reader and on the rulers of England. The same fear that besets England, Napoleon's large force, may cripple the Spanish, and it is answered in similar terms: "For present annoyancy his power is, no doubt, mighty: but liberty . . . is far mightier; and the good in human nature is stronger than the evil" (pp. 333–34) This is again a sentiment relying for its conviction simply on the repeated rhetorical pattern of the treatise.

With this statement *Cintra* is completed. A perspective has been created in terms of which the details of the Convention, the power of Napoleon, the actions of Spanish authorities and English politicians, and the responses of the peoples of Spain, England, and Portugal are consistently interpreted: the perspective of the human passion for justice and for faith in the victory of the good. The main task of *Cintra* was to develop this perspective within the reader, rather than to offer specific suggestions for military or political action. As Wordsworth declares in a summarizing statement of his procedure: before a course of "practical" action could be suggested,

it was first necessary to examine the grounds of hope in the grand and disinterested passions, and in the laws of universal morality. My attention has therefore been chiefly directed to these laws and passions; *in order to elevate, in some degree, the conceptions of my readers; and with a wish to rectify and fix, in this fundamental point, their judgements*. (p. 338, my italics)

Convention of Cintra was Wordsworth's most sustained and ambitious attempt to effect such complex changes in his reader.

The attempt was not entirely successful. His rhetorical compulsiveness, his desire to use every sentence as an exercise for the reader's sensibility, left no place for the comparative relaxation of historical analysis and illustration or even for a formal defense of the assumptions of his argument. These characteristics, as Coleridge noted, particularly doomed the work with the public of 1809, "effeminated, as it is, by the unremitting Action of great outward Events daily soliciting & daily gratifying the appetite of Curiosity."[18]

This remark anticipates the dangers Coleridge was to discover in the "experiment" of *The Friend*, which similarly asked its readers "to retire *into themselves* and make their own minds the objects of their stedfast attention"; and which similarly sought to revitalize the reader's sense of principle ("the [old] Topics, Evil and Good") rather than gratify "the cravings of curiosity" with the immediate and the novel. (Perhaps with *Cintra* in mind, Coleridge sought to simplify his style and to offer "occasional interludes, and vacations of innocent entertainment and promiscuous information."[19]) The goals of both works and the obstacles to their success recall an earlier literary "experiment."

Lyrical Ballads had sought to increase the reader's capability "of being excited without the application of the gross and violent stimulants" provided by the events of the day. Wordsworth's trust of 1800 in "certain inherent and indestructible qualities of the human mind" as more durable than the current "craving for extraordinary incidents" was still evident in his prose text of nearly a decade later. The very weaknesses of *Cintra*, the great beached whale of romantic prose, are conspicuous testimony to Wordsworth's preoccupation with turning passive readers into self-reflecting and self-energizing participants, a preoccupation so great as finally to deny him at

18. Letter of 22 June 1809 to Thomas W. Smith. *Letters of Coleridge*, vol. 3, 217.

19. *The Friend*, ii, 73, 150–51, 273, 276.

times a clear insight of an appropriate style and tone in achieving his goal.

✲   ✲   ✲

With Samuel Johnson's "Essay on Epitaphs" as a point of contrast, a brief glance at "Essays upon Epitaphs" (1810) will serve as summary and as conclusion to our examination of Wordsworth's dealings with his prose readership. Johnson viewed the genre of epitaph in terms of its final cause: "to perpetuate the examples of virtue, that the tomb of a good man may supply the want of his presence, and veneration for his memory produce the same effect as the observation of his life."[20] Thus, for Johnson the most perfect epitaph is the one "best adapted to exalt the reader's ideas and rouse his emulation," and the "Essay" is appropriately structured as a series of directives for achieving this "adaptation." The praise of the deceased, for example, ought not to be general:

> When we hear only of a good or great man, we know not in what class to place him, nor have any notion of his character, distinct from that of a thousand others; his example can have no effect upon our conduct, as we have nothing remarkable or eminent to propose to our limitation.

Further, the best subject of an epitaph is "private virtue; virtue exerted in the same circumstances in which the bulk of mankind are placed, and which, therefore, may admit of many imitators." In short, Johnson's brief essay is a guide for *authors* of epitaphs in ordering their productions to their appropriate ends. In terms of his dealings with his own reader, although the editorial "we" is employed throughout the "Essay," Johnson does not seek a particularly close or personal bond; the organization is deductive rather than rhetorical: once having determined the final cause of epitaphs, Johnson proceeds with specific recommendations on the basis of that final cause.

20. Johnson's essay was published in the December 1740 issue of *The Gentleman's Magazine*. My text is from *The Works of Samuel Johnson*, ed. Arthur Murphy, vol. 2 (London, 1801), 270–80.

Wordsworth's focus in his discussion of the genre is on the *reader* of epitaphs, to whom he closely and constantly attends throughout the three essays: "I invite the Reader to indulge with me," "the purpose of [my] remarks . . . was chiefly to assist the reader," "I now solicit the Reader's attention,"[21] and so on. His method is the citation and analysis of numerous examples — successful and unsuccessful — of the genre. Somewhat reminiscent of the "primitivism" of certain passages in the "Preface to *Lyrical Ballads*," Wordsworth begins with the most rude, direct, and general statements of faith in immortality, such as might be found in rural churchyards, rather than with artful and sophisticated epitaphs. The reason for this procedure betrays the central purpose of the "Essays": to enable his reader the more easily to "[participate] the truths upon which these general attestations were founded"; and

> to bring the ingenuous into still closer communion with those *primary sensations of the human heart*, which are the vital springs of sublime and pathetic composition, in this and in every other kind. And, as from these *primary sensations* such composition speaks, so, unless *correspondent ones listen promptly and submissively in the inner cell of the mind to whom it is addressed*, the voice cannot be heard: its highest powers are wasted. (my italics)[22]

In short, as in the *Cintra* pamphlet, Wordsworth wants the reader to become conscious of certain dispositions in himself, specifically here the imaginatively religious sentiments that are the source of the power and quality of the poetic texts being examined. Just as in the "Preface to Lyrical Ballads," in Hazlitt's lecture on "Poetry in General," and — as we will shortly see — in Coleridge's *Essays on the Principles of Genial Criticism*, the reader of "Essays on Epitaphs" is asked to recognize and to activate his own poetic temperament as the basis for literary judgment and response. Sincerity is, for Wordsworth, the inevitable test of the

21. *Prose Works of Wordsworth*, vol. 2, 49n, 53, 82.
22. Ibid., 68, 70.

writer of epitaphs: has he been faithful to "those primary sensations of the human heart"? To develop a "test of inward simplicity," one must exercise "habits of reflection"; he continues, "I am now writing with a hope of assisting the well-disposed to attain it."[23]

The actual argumentation of the "Essays" is less subtle, complex, or interesting than the dealings with the reader found in *Cintra* or in the "Preface." Despite the close relationship between reader and writer, the "Essays" are content to be expository and assertive. The reader's "participation" is assumed, not engineered.[24] Still, in thematic terms the reader remains Wordsworth's central concern here as in the other two works we have examined. All three in their various ways establish Wordsworth's endorsement of one of the original impulses in the enterprise of romantic prose.

23. Ibid., 70.
24. See, for example, Wordsworth's discussion of George Lord Lyttleton's epitaph for his wife:
This Epitaph would derive little advantage from being translated into another style . . . for there is no under current, no skeleton or stamina, of thought and feeling. The Reader will perceive at once that nothing in the heart of the Writer had determined either the choice, the order, or the expression, of the ideas — that there is no interchange of action from within and from without — that the connections are mechanical and arbitrary, and the lowest kind of these — Heart and Eyes — petty alliterations, as meek and magnanimous, witty and wise, combined with oppositions in thoughts where there is no necessary or natural opposition. (II, 75)

5. COLERIDGE AND THE READER

None of the romantic prose writers displayed a more intense and lifelong preoccupation with his readership than Samuel Taylor Coleridge, nor did any employ more diverse modes of discourse to stimulate an appropriate response to the prose process.[1] Although, as we shall see, the role of the reader in Coleridge's prose underwent a general redefinition and redirection sometime before 1809, the nature of the reader-writer relationship throughout Coleridge's career was always conditioned by the purposes of particular texts and the demands of specific audiences. Political editorials and "popular" addresses employed quite different tactics than were to be found in speculations on philosophy, religion, and aesthetics. Thus, works as distant in time as *Conciones ad Populum* (1795) and *The Statesman's Manual* (1816) share identical rhetorical strategies that set them apart from such intervening texts as *The Friend* (1809–10) or the *Essays on the Principles of Genial Criticism* (1814). A study of selected Coleridge texts will reveal a wide range of procedures for shaping the reader's role and response — from a fairly strict following of traditional "public" discourse to modes of prose requiring the virtual abandonment or annihilation of such dis-

1. Coleridge's relations with his readers have received considerable attention in recent years, particularly with reference to *Biographia Literaria*. See M. G. Cooke, "*Quisque Sui Faber*: Coleridge in the *Biographia Literaria*," 208–29; R. Mallette, "Narrative Technique and Structure in the *Biographia Literaria*," 32–40; and Kathleen M. Wheeler's excellent study *Sources, Processes and Methods in Coleridge's Biographia Literaria*. Jerome Christensen's *Coleridge's Blessed Machine of Language* deals with the problem of communication in both the *Biographia* and the 1818 edition of *The Friend*. A more general treatment of the subject, but a useful one, is James A. Berlin's "The Rhetoric of Romanticism: The Case for Coleridge," *Rhetoric Society Quarterly* 10 (1980): 62–74.

course and often quite literally disappearing into poetry or into the silence of contemplation and vision.

⁂   ⁂   ⁂

> The love of truth conjoined with a keen delight in a strict, skilful, yet impassioned argumentation, is my master-passion. — Coleridge's annotation to *Letters of Junius* [2]

In our desire to find all modes of romantic literary expression to be radically innovative, it is well to know that in prose the romantics were thoroughly trained in the firmly established tradition of classical rhetoric, like Milton, Sidney, and most other writers in the western world were for nearly two thousand years. Classical rhetoric had originally been conceived, and was most frequently employed, for discourses on public issues. In this regard we should remember that politics is the largest single subject in the varied body of romantic prose. Wordsworth's statement of 1833 that he had given "twelve hours thought to the conditions and prospects of society, for one of poetry" [3] is supported by the high percentage of political writing in his collected prose, from the early "Letter to the Bishop of Llandaff" through *Kendal and Windermere Railway* more than fifty years later; and this same emphasis is found in the writings of Coleridge, Hazlitt, Shelley, and Southey, among the major authors.

Intensive reading of the classical rhetoricians was traditionally the province of the university. Hazlitt attended lectures on Quintilian at the Unitarian New College at Hackney and presumably received practice in constructing the classical oration, for the policy at Hackney was that "at the end of every session there were public proceedings at which students delivered 'Orations' in English and Latin." [4] Aristotle dominated the

---

2. *Coleridge's Miscellaneous Criticism*, ed. Thomas M. Raysor, p. 315.

3. Orville Dewey, *The Old World and the New* (1836), as quoted in F. M. Todd, *Politics and the Poet: A Study of Wordsworth* (London: Methuen, 1957), p. 11.

4. H. McLachlan, *English Education under the Test Acts* (Manchester, England: University of Manchester Press, 1931), p. 252. See also Hazlitt's letters

curriculum at Oxford, and the final examination for which De Quincey had to prepare in 1808 required a "perfect mastery of the minuter details of logic, ethics, and rhetoric."[5]

Mathematics had to a considerable extent supplanted classical studies at Cambridge, but the orations of Demosthenes were still the subject matter for examination during Wordsworth's days at St. John's.[6] As Christopher Wordsworth notes, Aristotle, Thucydides, and Cicero were also studied, and for a purpose: "The *thesis* which opened every Respondency in the Schools or in College Chapels, gave an opening for exercise therein, and the same purpose was yet better served by the College *Declamations*."[7] Coleridge's letters from Jesus College (1791–1794) speak of his preparation for these declamations; of the praise he received for one delivered in early 1792 on the topic "That the desire of Posthumous Fame is unworthy a Wise Man"; and of his composing one in 1794 for his friend Robert Allen "on the comparative good and Evil of Novels."[8]

However, the influence of certain aspects of classical rhetoric was manifested even earlier, in the grammar-school training

---

to his father from Hackney in 1793 (*The Hazlitts: An Account of their Origin and Descent*, ed. W. Carew Hazlitt, pp. 399–403).

Hazlitt's absorption of classical rhetoric is clear from the critical notes to his collection *The Eloquence of the British Senate* (1807), in which he quotes and repeatedly applies Quintilian's dictum that "passion makes men eloquent." See *The Complete Works of William Hazlitt*, ed. P. P. Howe, vol. 1, 145, 147, 153–54; VII, 297–300, 313–17.

5. James Hogg, *De Quincey and his Friends* (London, 1895), p. 109.

6. Ben Ross Schneider, Jr., *Wordsworth's Cambridge Education* (Cambridge University Press, 1957), p. 156. Wordsworth had purchased a copy of Demosthenes while still at Hawkshead, possibly in preparation for his university studies (Mark L. Reed, *Wordsworth: The Chronology of the Early Years 1770–1799* [Cambridge, Mass.: Harvard University Press, 1967], p. 68).

7. *Scholae Academicae: Some Account of the Studies at the English Universities in the Eighteenth Century* (Cambridge, England: Cambridge University Press, 1910), p. 88.

8. *The Collected Letters of Samuel Taylor Coleridge*, ed. Earl Leslie Griggs, vol. 1, 17, 24, 71. For the text of the declamation on "the desire of Posthumous Fame," see Anthony John Harding, "Coleridge's College Declamation, 1792," pp. 361–67.

in Latin and English composition. The basic text studied by Coleridge, Lamb, and Leigh Hunt, James Penn's *Latin Grammar for the Use of Christ's Hospital* (1761), contained an appendix of figures of speech and rhetoric that were to adorn the essays. The essays themselves, usually on some moral topic, were constructed by following the precepts formulated in the *Ad Herennium* and passed down through various Latin and English composition manuals:

> after having expressed the theme simply, we can subjoin the Reason, and then express the theme in another form, with or without the Reasons; next we can present the Contrary . . . then a Comparison and an Example . . . and finally the Conclusion.[9]

Seven of Coleridge's essays written at Christ's Hospital have been preserved,[10] and they illustrate his mastery of this rhetorical principle of *expolitio*. The first of these, dated 6 June 1788, opens with a statement of the theme: "Temperance is the first step towards making our life happy." Then follows the reason: "For from Health, which is the natural effect of this Virtue, do we derive the enjoyment of all other advantages." Coleridge then provides an example:

9. *Ad Herennium*, IV.xliii.56–58. All quotations from *Ad Herennium* are from the translation by Harry Caplan, Loeb Classical Library (Cambridge: Harvard University Press — London: William Heinemann, 1954).

In his somewhat humorous recollection of the process of composition-writing at Christ's Hospital, Leigh Hunt affirms the persistence of the tradition:

You wrote out the subject very fairly at top, *Quid non mortalia*, etc., or *Crescit amor nummi*. Then the ingenious thing was to repeat this apophthegm in as many words and roundabout phrases as possible, which took up a good bit of the paper. Then you attempted to give a reason or two, why *amor nummi* was bad; or on what accounts heroes ought to eschew ambition; after which naturally came a few examples, got out of Plutarch or the *Selectae e Profanis*; and the happy moralist concluded with signing his name. (*The Autobiography of Leigh Hunt*, ed. J. E. Morpurgo, p. 78).

10. In James Boyer's "Liber Aureus" (British Museum, Ashley Ms. 3506). Only two of these — the essays of September 1790 and of 19 January 1791 — have heretofore been published (*Illustrated London News* [1 April 1893]: p. 398; Lawrence Hanson, *The Life of S. T. Coleridge: The Early Years* [London: Oxford University Press, 1938], pp. 424–25).

The most exquisite viands become tasteless, and disgusting to one labouring under the gout, or any other painful, but usual effect of excess. Whilst Appetite renders the most simple food a delicacy to the temperate Husbandman.

The succeeding two paragraphs, citing the bodily and mental results of temperance, present further reasons for the proposition. The fourth paragraph then presents the contrary:

But it is impossible, that Reason should dwell in the mind of the Luxurious; over whom the Passions have absolute Command. For how could it preserve it's necessary authority, when the Body is debilitated by Disease, and the unruly Appetites inflamed to Madness by Wine!

The essay concludes with a similitude:

Thus, like a Ship driven by Whirlwinds, the intemperate man drives on from one excess to another, till at last he splits on the Rock of Infamy, or falls a sacrifice to Poverty and Despair. Whilst Temperance, like a skilful Pilot, guides her followers safe from all these Misfortunes to Honour, Peace, and Happiness.

One of the most widely used grammar-school texts of the period provides further testimony to the presence of classical rhetoric in the curriculum. The student probably first encountered Quintilian in Jean Heuzet's *Selectae e Profanis Scriptoribus Historiae*,[11] an anthology of very short selections from the Roman writers used in the third or fourth year for translation exercises and as a source of topics for English and Latin themes. Coleridge certainly seems to have used Heuzet's text in this latter way in his essay on the careful attention to the education of youth (November 1788). The second section of the *Selectae* contained an entry on the topic *Maxima debetur puero reverentia*, which was illustrated with quotations from Juvenal's four-

11. First published in France in the early eighteenth century, *Selectae e Profanis* saw London editions of 1775, 1780, 1784, 1796, 1801, 1806, and 1832. Editions were published in Philadelphia in 1787, 1809, and 1819.

teenth Satire, from Quintilian, and from Aulus Gellius. In what may constitute his first literary borrowing or plagiarism, Coleridge opens the essay with the same quotation from Juvenal and subsequently paraphrases the excerpt from Quintilian.

All this suggests that classical rhetoric was still very much a part of the education of Coleridge and the other romantic writers. Indeed, Byron spoke for most of his contemporaries when in 1807 he included Demosthenes, Cicero, and Quintilian among those writers he knew so well that he could "quote passages from any mentioned."[12] It is not surprising, therefore, that when the romantics came to write works of persuasive prose on public issues, classical rhetoric constituted one widely accepted way of addressing the reader and shaping his response to the text.

The most obvious evidence of classical rhetoric is, of course, stylistic. One does not have to turn many pages of Coleridge's political writings before coming across examples of *anadiplosis*, *anaphora*, *antimetabole*, *climax*, *epiphonema*, *epistrophe*, and *isocolon*, etc.[13] — many of which were listed among the twenty-seven figures of speech and fifty figures of rhetoric in the *Christ's Hospital Latin Grammar*. However, the influence of classical rhetoric is found in more significant areas than *elocutio*. I refer to the arrangement of the entire discourse (*dispositio*) or the kinds of arguments employed (*inventio*).

Coleridge's earliest published prose, *Conciones ad Populum* (1795),[14] reveals a thorough familiarity with these procedures of classical rhetoric and their time-honored mixture of logical, ethical, and emotional appeals to the reader; indeed, the second of the *Conciones*, "On the Present War," might almost be a model of such procedures. This *forensic* address observes the following *dispositio*: an exordium including the statement of the proposi-

12. *The Works of Lord Byron: with his Letters and Journals and his Life*, ed. Thomas Moore, vol. 1, 143.

13. See *Essays on his Times*, ed. David V. Erdman, in *Collected Works of Coleridge*, vol. 3, i, 7, 15, 20, 22, 24, 43, 45.

14. *Lectures 1795 on Politics and Religion*, ed. Lewis Patton and Peter Mann, vol. 1 (1971) of *Works of Coleridge*. All quotations from *Conciones* are from this edition, which will be cited in my text hereafter by page number.

tion that the present war is evil (paragraphs 1–3); a refutation of the charge that the war was just and necessary (paragraphs 4–6); a confirmation of the proposition by the topos of consequences (paragraphs 7–19); and a final paragraph of recapitulation and peroration.

Coleridge appropriately employs the exordium to render his readers "well-disposed, attentive and receptive." To achieve the first of these goals, he draws from each of the sources of goodwill described in Cicero's *De Inventione* — "from our own person, from the person of the opponents, from the persons of the jury [the auditors], and from the case itself."[15]

"In the disclosal of Opinion," the *Concion* begins,

> it is our duty to consider the character of those, to whom we address ourselves, their situations, and probable degree of knowledge. We should be bold in the avowal of *political* Truth among those only whose minds are susceptible of reasoning: and never to the multitude, who ignorant and needy must necessarily act from the impulse of inflamed Passions.

In contrast to his prudent and judicious behavior in "[preserving] this distinction," Coleridge refers to the irresponsible behaviour of the "Child of Prejudice and the Slave of Corruption," who will

> industriously represent it as confounded: whatever may be the sentiments and language of the present Address, the *attempt* to promote Discussion will be regarded as dangerous, and from fools and from bigots I shall be honoured with much complimentary Reviling, and many panegyrical Abuses.

To these unjust opponents, he replies:

> But the Conduct of the speaker is determined chiefly by the nature of his Audience. He therefore, who shall proclaim me *seditious* because I speak "against wickedness in high

15. I.xvi.22. Cicero, *De Inventione, De Optimo Genere Oratorum Topica*, trans. H. M. Hubbell, Loeb Classical Library, (Harvard University Press — London: William Heinemann, 1976).

places," must prove the majority of my hearers to be un-
enlightened, and therefore easily deluded — or Men of des-
perate fortunes, and therefore eager for the *Scramble* of a
Revolution. (pp. 51–52)

In this first paragraph, Coleridge has combined three of the
four sources recommended by Cicero: he has asserted his own
prudent and responsible character; he has shown the irrespon-
sibility of his opponents in abusing him; and he has compli-
mented his audience on their "enlightened" character. These
appeals are all expanded in the second and third paragraphs. In
a final statement of the exordium, referring to the importance of
the case itself, Coleridge simultaneously consolidates the goodwill, attentiveness and receptivity of his readers: "This Duty [of
forming and propagating one's opinions about the state of one's
country] we should exert at all times, but with peculiar ardor in
seasons of public Calamity, when there exists an Evil of such
incalculable magnitude as the PRESENT WAR" (pp. 53–54).

The subject, "a comprehensive view" of the "peculiar crimes
and distresses" of the war, is then announced and dealt with extensively in paragraphs seven to nineteen. But first Coleridge
must refute the notion that the war was "just and necessary";
for "if the War had been just and necessary, it might be thought
disputable whether any Calamities could justify our abandonment of it." He initially makes his point that the war was unjust
and unnecessary by the following enthymemic reasoning: "The
War might probably have been prevented by Negociation: Negociation was never attempted. It cannot therefore be *proved*
to have been a *necessary* war, and consequently it is not a just
one" (p. 54).

A refutation of the various reasons offered by the British
government for not negotiating then follows. I shall deal here
only with the final and climactic procedure of refutation. Coleridge makes a comparison between the situations of England
vs. France and the American colonies vs. England, employing
the common topos of *a fortiori* in asking, if the colonists, who
suffered hideous atrocities at the hands of the British, did not
refuse to negotiate, why should we, who have less provocation,

refuse to negotiate with the French? An impassioned description follows of the happy paradise of the American settlers laid waste by Indians under the instigation of British authorities. Yet, despite these provocations, as Coleridge states, "these high-minded Republicans did not refuse to negociate with us" (pp. 55–59).

Having completed the refutation that the war against France was necessary and just, Coleridge now turns to the confirmation of the evil of the war through consideration of its consequences. Following an extended instance of *paralipsis* (p. 59), he deals with these consequences at length (pp. 60–73) in an order of ascending gravity: the loss of our national character; the devastation of private morals; the threats to liberty produced by the suspension of the Habeas Corpus and by other actions of William Pitt; the economic hardships of the poor of England, leading them to crime and eventually to punishment by banishment or death, this in turn provoking the government to "crimping" and other measures to sustain the military forces; and the excesses of the French, "their massacres and blasphemies, all their crimes and all their distresses," caused by the British continuation of the war.

The concluding paragraph of the *Concion* illustrates the two aspects of a peroration discussed at length by Quintilian, the recapitulation of the facts or arguments and the emotional appeal. A recapitulation

> serves both to refresh the memory of the judge and to place the whole of the case before his eyes, and, even although the facts may have made little impression on him in detail, their cumulative effect is considerable.

Quintilian further recommends that the recapitulation be brief, yet "the points selected for enumeration must be treated with weight and dignity, enlivened by apt reflexions and diversified by suitable figures."[16] Coleridge writes:

16. VI.i.1–2. *The Institutio Oratoria of Quintilian*, trans. H. E. Butler, 4 vols., Loeb Classical Library, (Harvard University Press — London: William Heinemann, 1966–1968).

> Our national faith has been impaired; our social confidence
> hath been weakened, or made unsafe; our liberties have suf-
> fered a perilous breach, and even now are being (still more
> perilously) undermined; the Dearth, which would otherwise
> have been scarcely visible, hath enlarged its terrible features
> into the threatening face of Famine; and finally, of US will
> justice require a dreadful account of whatever guilt France
> has perpetrated, of whatever miseries France has endured.
> (p. 74)

The last of these charges, with the emphasized "US," begins
the second aspect of peroration mentioned by Quintilian, the
emotional appeal. According to all classical rhetoricians, such
an appeal has its place throughout the oration, but most especially in the conclusion. Here the appeal takes the form of
"Arousal," [17] as Coleridge poses the challenge, "Are we men?
Freemen? rational men? And shall we carry on this wild and
priestly War against reason, against freedom, against human
nature?" Coleridge concluded the *Concion* with a powerful *epiphonema*, "If there be one among you, who departs from me
without feeling it his immediate duty to petition or remonstrate
against the continuance of it, I envy that man neither his head
or his heart!"

Such an unswerving accommodation of argument to the
procedures of classical rhetoric can be found also in *The Statesman's Manual* (1816) [18] and in the two pamphlets of 1818 on the
child labor laws. Quite clearly classical rhetoric was a mode of
discourse to which Coleridge freely turned whenever the occasion, subject, or audience made it appropriate. However, it
should be noted that the first of the *Conciones* of 1795 already
shows Coleridge's tendency toward a quite different kind of discourse, one that eventually dominated much of his important
prose more than twenty years later. To be sure, the "Introduc-

---

17. "When not only we ourselves seem to speak under emotion, but we
also stir the hearer" (*Ad Herennium*, IV.xliii.55).

18. For a detailed rhetorical analysis, see my "Romantic Prose and Classical Rhetoric," pp. 123–25.

tory Address" reveals in its style, organization, and argumentation the familiar tactics of the rhetorical tradition we have documented at length in its companion *Concion*,[19] but the *nature* and *direction* of the argument and the response sought from the reader are very different.

The proposition of the *deliberative* "Address" — developed through traditional appeals to the "useful" and the "honorable" and with an extended confirmation by example — is the necessity for a moral reformation in the poorer classes as the precondition for their experience of political freedom, and for the cultivation of "benevolent affections" in the already enlightened zealots of freedom who hope to assist this reformation. The "Address" is thus directed to changes of character rather than of opinion, to self-examination rather than external action. The concluding paragraph contains a significant metaphor revealing exactly the internal movement that is both the impulse and the fulfillment of the argument: "It is not enough that we have swallowed these Truths — we must feed on them, as insects on a leaf, till the whole heart be coloured by their qualities, and shew its food in every the minutest fibre" (p. 48). Coleridge asks of his reader an activity of meditation beyond the immediate argument and rhetoric of the text.[20]

This early concern to address the reader on a deeper level than classical rhetoric ordinarily sought to reach, and to require of him an active response and exertion of thought and self-reflection, becomes the paramount rhetorical procedure of Coleridge's mature prose from the time of *The Friend* (1809–1810), which is the central document for understanding Coleridge's original contribution to the reader-writer relationship in ro-

19. Ibid., pp. 120–22.
20. On the conclusion of the "Address," see David R. Sanderson, "Coleridge's Political 'Sermons,'" p. 325.

For another early example of Coleridge's political prose directing itself to a moral or religious change in the reader, see the "Lecture on the Slave Trade" delivered in Bristol 16 June 1795 and printed in *The Watchman* the following year. (*Lectures 1795 on Politics and Religion*, pp. 235–51; *The Watchman*, ed. Lewis Patton, vol. 2 [1970] of *Collected Works of Coleridge*, pp. 130–40).

mantic prose. Before turning to that text, I should like to consider still another early composition that reveals the writer's concern to engage his reader in a process of self-examination. This time the concern is not with political action or opinion but with habits of reading poetry. I refer to the unpretentious little "Preface" to *Poems on Various Subjects, By S. T. Coleridge* (1796).[21]

The "Preface" moves from the defense by the poet of his poetic texts to a forthright instruction in the proper reading of those texts. The initial charge of "egotism" against the monodies and sonnets that comprise the volume is readily answered in terms of genre: "egotism" is as appropriate to such forms as it would be inappropriate in history or in epic verse. The second charge is against choosing these forms at all, and this is answered in terms of their therapeutic effect on the suffering poet:

> The communicativeness of our Nature leads us to describe our own sorrows; in the endeavour to describe them, intellectual activity is exerted; and from intellectual activity there results a pleasure, which is gradually associated, and mingles as a corrective, with the painful subject of the description.

A third charge immediately follows: "But how are the PUBLIC interested in your Sorrows or your Description?" Whereas the second charge was answered in terms of the writer, this final charge is answered in terms of the pleasure imparted to the readers, "of whom as many will be interested in these sorrows, as have experienced the same or similar." In short, the character and the experience of the reader are assimilated to the poet's.

Having thus attempted to unite the "Public" with him against his critics, Coleridge then turns from defense and refutation to offense and instruction. The truly condemnable egotists are the critics who earlier condemned the poet's verses. Those who

---

21. I follow the revised text of "Preface to the First Edition" as it appeared in *Poems, by S. T. Coleridge, Second Edition, in which are now added Poems by Charles Lamb, and Charles Lloyd* (1797). A modern reprint of the "Preface" can be found in *The Complete Poetical Works of Samuel Taylor Coleridge*, ed. Ernest Hartley Coleridge, vol. 2, 1144–45.

"would reduce the feelings of others to an identity with their own" are guilty of egotism; "The sleek Favorites of Fortune are Egotists, when they condemn all 'melancholy, discontented' verses." Having turned the tables on his critics in this circular fashion, Coleridge directly cautions his reader to suspect his own judgment in responding to these poems rather than to criticize the character of the poet:

> each of my readers will, I hope, remember that these Poems on various subjects, which he reads at one time and under the influence of one set of feelings, were written at different times and prompted by very different feelings; and therefore that the supposed inferiority of one Poem to another may sometimes be owing to the temper of mind, in which he happens to peruse it.

Although its subject is literature rather than politics, the "Preface" of 1796 shares with the "Introductory Address" of the previous year a concern with provoking self-reflection in its reader. In the "Address" the purpose is to prepare the "enlightened" reader for effective public action; in the "Preface" the purpose is to expand the range of his literary responsiveness and human sympathy.

These somewhat tentative and certainly brief attempts to bring the prose reader to an act of self-examination were climaxed with the publication of *The Friend*, which appeared as a periodical of twenty-seven issues in 1809 and 1810, then as a one-volume collection in 1812, and finally as a very substantially revised three-volume edition in 1818. The work is clearly of major importance in Coleridge's career as a writer: it employs in an extended publication a form of prose designed to provoke an act of self-reflection that Coleridge had come to see as essential for discourse on questions of philosophical complexity or of moral significance. A remark in a letter of 1806 is premonitory: in explaining to Thomas Clarkson the difference between "thought" and "things," he declared that his ideal reader in such a difficult endeavor would be one "who *seeks* to understand, and looks into himself for a sense, which my words may excite in him, not *to* my words for a sense, which they must against his will *force* on him."[22]

The Friend three years later was an "experiment"[23] to see if there were a sufficient number of such readers and also if prose could be effectively shaped for such purposes. The subject matter itself was not novel; it involved, as Coleridge admitted, the oldest of topics, the presence of good and evil in man's nature and the question of conscience and free will. The purpose of the text was to precipitate a heightened awareness of these central facts of our moral life. "Genuine self-research" must be the method; only "by [retiring] *into themselves* and [making] their own minds the objects of their stedfast attention" could readers of *The Friend* arrive at freshened conviction about these internal "realities" (pp. 8, 151). The periodical version of 1809– 1810, for all its chaotic history of publication and its often maddening mixture of materials, is worth examining as its author's first full-scale attempt at the procedures in romantic prose we have been tracing in this study.

In fashioning a work that would stimulate the act of self-reflection, Coleridge was aware that a prerequisite would have to be the reader's more-than-usual trust in the writer. Accordingly, at the end of the first issue, he promises a full account of his opinions "on the delicate subjects of Religion and Politics." In addition to the obvious reason for this disclosure — that he may not mislead or deceive his reader in such important matters — he will also use the occasion to show his own self-reflective procedure of tracing opinions to the "root" principles of man's nature. However, before even these "delicate" matters are treated, a further concern mediating between reader and

---

22. *Letters of Coleridge*, vol. 2, 1194. For other early remarks about language and the problem of communication, see *Collected Letters of Coleridge*, vol. 1, 625–26; *The Notebooks of Samuel Taylor Coleridge*, ed. Kathleen Coburn, entries 1016, 1387. It should be noted that the closer one comes to the preparation and publication of *The Friend*, the more the references to the subject multiply: see entries 2152, 2998, 3242, 3268, 3287, 3302, 3401, 3549.

23. *The Friend*, ed. Barbara E. Rooke, in *Collected Works of Coleridge*, vol. 4, ii, 273–77. All references to the 1809–10 *Friend* will be given hereafter in my text by page number to the second volume of the Rooke edition.

writer must be addressed: the possible charge of arrogance lodged against the writer "for daring to dissent from the opinions of great Authorities . . . and from the general opinion concerning the true value of certain Authorities deemed great" (p. 32). This potential obstacle is treated extensively. Creating a strong bond between reader and writer is apparently — and inevitably — an overriding concern in a work that demands both "Thought," that is, the "voluntary production in our own minds of those states of consciousness, to which, as to his fundamental facts, the Writer has referred us," and "Attention," that is, "the order and connection of Thoughts and Images, each of which is in itself already and familiarly known" (p. 277).

Symptomatic of the entire work, Coleridge seeks to trace arrogance to "some definite Law." In this, as in all moral matters, the answer lies in the writer's intention and in the integrity of the principle that shapes the intention. Coleridge initially seeks to establish his own virtuous credentials by stating his intention not to offer original opinions "without condescending to prefix or annex the facts and reasons on which such opinions were formed"; not to attack "with the bitterness of personal crimination" the opponents of his opinions; lastly, not to advance "with all the high pretensions of originality, opinions and observations, in regard to which he must plead wilful Ignorance in order to be acquitted of dishonest Plagiarism" (pp. 33–34). Yet this passage of personal affirmation in issue two is but the preface to an endeavor extending over three installments (10 August, 7 September, 14 September) devoted to the analysis of "the Communication of Truth and the Rightful Liberty of the Press in connection with it," in which the "intention" is traced to "principles."

The topic has an experiential basis in Coleridge's "reflections" in the very act of composing the work before the reader:

> These reflections were forced on me by an accident during a short visit at a neighbouring house, as I was endeavouring to form some determinate principles of conduct in relation to my weekly labors — some rule which might guide my judg-

ment in the choice of my subjects and in my manner of treat-
ing them, and secure me from the disturbing forces of any
ungentle moods of my own temper . . . as well as from the
undue influence of passing events.

The immediate provocation was his accidental glance at an issue
of the *Edinburgh Review*, which precisely advocated the "expedient" practice of "pious frauds" in communication — "to intermix
falsehoods with truths . . . provided only they hereby serve the
interests of Truth and the advantage of mankind." In reply, Coleridge sought to prove

> that the more strictly we adhere to the *Letter* of the moral law
> in this respect, the more compleately shall we reconcile the
> law with prudence, and secure a purity in the principle with-
> out mischief from the practice. (pp. 39–41)

In presenting his proof, Coleridge drew a distinction between mere verbal truth and moral truth. In the latter "we . . .
involve the intention of the speaker, that his words should cor-
respond to his thoughts in the sense in which he expects them
to be understood." Then he questioned whether more than ve-
racity ("the truth and nothing but the truth") is demanded by
conscience, namely, simplicity ("the truth only, and the whole
truth"). This question involves not simply a "right" notion but
also a "complete" notion regardless of impediments in the listeners that might lead to distortion or misunderstanding
of the "whole truth." Conscience requires as a minimum always
a "right" notion, that is, no intermixture of falsehood with
truth; and when this minimum is not possible, then the speaker
must abstain from any attempt at communication. In all these
considerations, Coleridge drew on "the sole principle of Self-
consistence or moral Integrity." This section of argument closes
with an appeal to the reader, "whether he who most faithfully
adheres to the letter of the law of conscience" as outlined in the
preceding discussion "will not likewise act in strictest corre-
spondence to the maxims of prudence and sound policy."

The consideration of the question of "pious frauds," of adulterating truth for expedient gains, has not been reduced to a predictable argument by consequences, such as the fatally imprudent effects of Christian pastors mixing doctrine with superstition and thus "paganizing" Christianity; rather, it has been traced to the dictates of conscience, one of the root principles whose centrality Coleridge wished to advance throughout *The Friend*, as in the very act of describing his role in the writer-reader relationship. The same appeal to the integrity of the intention of the agent informs the ensuing discussion of libel (pp. 56–68).

There is yet another reason for this prolonged discussion, perhaps its final cause. The reception of truth instead of "expedient falsehoods" leads to "clearer conceptions in the understanding," which in turn lead to "[purer] Principles of Action . . . in the Will." Most human misery occurs, Coleridge argues, not through natural calamities but through moral weakness. The communication of knowledge is one appropriate means of clarifying vices and thus purifying "man's principles of moral election." Coleridge's ideal of communication is offered in an ecstatic passage:

> Were but a hundred men to combine a deep conviction that virtuous Habits may be formed by the very means by which knowledge is communicated, that men may be made better, not only in consequence, but *by* the mode and *in* the process, of instruction: were but a hundred men to combine that clear conviction of this, which I myself at this moment feel, even as I feel the certainty of my being, with the perseverance of a CLARKSON or a BELL, the promises of ancient prophecy would disclose themselves to our Faith, even as when a noble Castle hidden from us by an intervening mist, discovers itself by its reflection in the tranquil Lake, on the opposite shore of which we stand gazing. (pp. 69–70)

The crucial phrase "that men may be made better, not only in consequence but *by* the mode and *in* the process, of instruction" is the seminal principle of *The Friend* itself, which precisely seeks to revitalize through its own discourse the reader's engagement with the sources of his moral being, his conscience, and his free will. The treatment of the "Communication of Truth" has been an illustration of this principle in a full discursive cycle from Coleridge's glance at the pages of the *Edinburgh Review*, through a search for a principle in the decision of the conscience, to the assertion of the prudential success of this conscientious behavior.

Coleridge now presents what he admits is the most difficult section of *The Friend*, the discussion of the faculties of man — Sensation, Understanding, and Reason — and their separate properties, functions, and limitations. Sensation is man considered as perfect animal; Understanding has as its function "the [taking up of] the *passive affections* [of Sensation] into distinct Thought"; Reason is the source of "Ideas of its own formation and underived from material Nature." Prophetic of the shifts of discourse to be found in his other mature prose,[24] Coleridge's discussion of Sensation and Understanding differs dramatically in discourse from the presentation of Reason. The first two move toward more and more analytically precise definitions, to which the reader may give logical assent. For example,

Sensation

The most approved Definition of a living Substance is, that its vitality consists in the susceptibility of being acted upon by external stimulants joined to the necessity of re-action; and in the due balance of this action and re-action, the healthy state of Life consists. We must, however, further add the power of acquiring *Habits*, and Facilities by repetition. This being the generical idea of Life, is common to all living Beings; but taken exclusively, it designates the lowest Class, Plants and Plant Animals. An addition to the mechanism gives locomotion. A still costlier and more complex apparatus diversly organizes the impressions received from the external powers that fall promiscuously on the whole surface. . . . To

24. See Sanderson, pp. 322 ff.; and my discussion below of *Essays on the Principles of Genial Criticism*.

these *Organs* of sense we suppose (by analogy from our own experience) sensation attached, and these sensuous impressions acting on other parts of the Machine, framed for other stimulants included in the Machine itself, namely, the Organs of Appetite; and these again working on the instruments of locomotion, and of those by which the external substances corresponding to the sensuous impressions can be acted upon, (the Mouth, Teeth, Talons, &c.) constitute our whole idea of the perfect *Animal.* (pp. 75-76)

Contrastingly, the presentation of Reason does not proceed by definition and distinction. Its discourse is one of biblical echoes, rhetorical incantation, and poetic quotation, to which the reader can respond only by putting aside his logical and analytical faculty and by calling on a more "intuitive" and "poetic" capacity:

But God created Man in his own Image: to be the Image of his own Eternity and Infinity created he Man. He gave us Reason and with Reason Ideas of its own formation and underived from material Nature, self-consciousness, Principles, and above all, the Law of Conscience, which in the power of an holy and omnipotent Being *commands* us to attribute Reality — among the numerous Ideas mathematical or philosophical, which the Reason by the necessity of its own excellence, creates for itself — to those, (and those only) without which the Conscience would be baseless and contradictory; namely, to the Ideas of Soul, the Free Will, Immortality, and God. To God as the Reality of the Conscience and the Source of all Obligation; to Free Will, as the power of the human being to maintain the Obedience, which God through the Conscience has commanded, against all the might of Nature; and to the immortality of the Soul as a State in which the weal and woe of man shall be proportioned to his moral Worth.

With this Faith all Nature,

— — — — — —all the mighty World

of Eye and Ear— — — — — — — —

presents itself to us, now as the Aggregate *Materials* of Duty, and now as a Vision of the Most High revealing to us the mode, and time, and particular instance of applying and realizing that universal Rule, pre-established in the Heart of our Reason: as

> The lovely shapes and sounds intelligible
> Of that Eternal Language, which our God
> Utters: Who from Eternity doth teach
> Himself in all, and all things in Himself!
> (pp. 78–81)

In answer to the anticipated charge that such conceptions of Reason are "enthusiastic" and "unworldly," Coleridge argues that "systematic" vice such as he identifies with Napoleon, though ultimately limited in its power, can only be contested by "some combining Principle" such as Reason provides to unite "mixed and scattered Virtues" (pp. 82–84). With this ascension of the moral instinct, the first climax of *The Friend* has been reached. The results of the Enlightenment attack on Reason and on Conscience have found their discredited end in the devastation of the French Revolution and are more positively manifested in a lesser belief in "our measureless superiority in Good Sense to our Ancestors." If false theories have now less credence, "thought" and "reflection" on the principles of *The Friend* would seem to be an appropriate means of recovery. Moreover, the spread of education has made any other means secondary:

> In an Age in which artificial knowledge is received almost at the Birth, Intellect and Thought alone can be our Upholder and Judge. Let the Importance of this Truth procure pardon for its repetition. Only by means of Seriousness and Meditation and the free infliction of Censure in the spirit of Love, can the true Philanthropist of the present Time, curb in himself and his Contemporaries; only by these can he aid in preventing the Evils which threaten us, not from the terrors of an Enemy so much as from *our fears of our own Thoughts, and our aversion to all the toils of Reflection*. (pp. 85–86; my italics)

With the end of the sixth issue (21 September 1809), Coleridge has attempted to establish the relationship of reader and writer; he has described the faculties of man on which his future argument will be based; and he has demonstrated the urgency and appropriateness of self-reflection. The initial issues of *The Friend* have themselves illustrated or applied each of these topics in the act of discursively presenting them.

The remainder of *The Friend* is, comparatively speaking, much less tidily controlled. There is, to be sure, the long-deferred presentation of Coleridge's political philosophy illustrating the preceding principles; a critique of Paley's theory of "general consequences" as a guide to morality (8 February 1810) and an essay "On the Law of Nations" (15 February 1810) are also executed in terms of those principles. But there is also such miscellaneous material as "Specimens of Rabbinical Wisdom," Satyrane's letters, Wordsworth's essay on epitaphs and the letter to Mathetes; all these haphazardly fill up the numbers, however much they are loosely connected as varying instances of psychological exploration and moral instruction.

Balancing the somewhat scrappy exposition, one strongly integrative subject is gradually developed in the later numbers. This involves a switch to the genre of biography. "Sketches and Fragments of the Life and Character of the Late Admiral Sir Alexander Ball" occupy four of the concluding issues, with anticipatory references in earlier issues. So integral did Coleridge consider this material that the "Sketches" were preserved as the concluding chapters of the much more orderly 1818 edition of *The Friend*. He evidently intended that the worldly applicability of the self-reflective moral endeavor of his work would be solidified with the record of a successful life conducted in strict accordance with the "root Truths," which are enunciated from the start of the publication. Indeed, Coleridge is explicit in acknowledging that his account of Ball contained "that connection with general Principles, by which . . . I would wish that every Number of THE FRIEND should be more or less marked" (pp. 298–99).

The very first anonymous reference to Ball (28 September 1809) makes the central point of the connection, that discipline on Ball's ship reposed on his appealing to and calling into operation

> the aweful power of LAW . . . a Faculty and a Presence [in the erring sailor], of which he had not been previously made aware — but it *answered* to the appeal! its real Existence therefore could not be doubted, or its reply rendered inaudible! (pp. 100–101)

A subsequent illustration of the principles of *The Friend* comes in Ball's belief that "no Body of Men can for any length of time be safely treated otherwise than as rational Beings" (p. 288). Even his fondness for Wordsworth's "Peter Bell" revealed his self-reflective bias: the poem represented for him an account of "various accidents which may awaken the most brutalized Person to a recognition of his nobler Being" (p. 290). In his taste, as in matters of military discipline and civil administration, Ball "lived as we should all live; and I doubt not, left the world as we should all wish to leave it" (p. 255), in full accord with the self-reflective activity to which the reader has been called from the start of *The Friend*.

°   °   °

The Friend of 1809–1810 is more significant for its attempt to reach a goal of prose expression than for its immaculate achievement of that goal. Literary devices such as the use of the autobiographical mode of self-reflection, the stylistic shifts to thwart a "logical" response to exposition and to argument, and the careful cultivation of a "friendly" persona whose processes of thought the reader is asked to duplicate, were more finely honed and disciplined in the later achievements of *Biographia Literaria* and in the 1818 edition of *The Friend*, as Kathleen M. Wheeler and Jerome Christensen have recently shown. I shall not attempt to add anything to their extensive and stimulating treatments of these works.

Of the remaining Coleridge texts, *Aids to Reflection* (1825) might seem an inescapable subject for my examination. Formally, it is a series of aphorisms, "notebook jottings," if you will. Each aphorism is followed by its appropriate "reflection," which is intended as a stimulus for the reader's own mental activity. One might conclude that Coleridge has here perfected the method he had first sought more than fifteen years earlier. Yet the very formality of the procedure — aphorism, reflection, aphorism, reflection, etc., all neatly arranged in an ascending order from prudential to moral and religious to spiritual topics — is a far less adventurous and intriguing example of Coleridge's dealings with his reader than the methods adopted in other texts we have examined. Wheeler makes the point when she notes that *Aids to Reflection* is organized "in a more conventionally acceptable format, at the expense however of imaginative power and effect. . . . The 1809–10 *Friend*, on the other hand, functions in an opposite sense from the *Aids* . . . in that it is a tentative, probing, and struggling effort toward the achievement of a method sustainedly artistic and dramatic. . . ."[25]

✿　　✿　　✿

Among Coleridge's later writings a more valuable instance is a work of 1814 entitled *Essays on the Principles of Genial Criticism concerning the Fine Arts, more especially those of Statuary and Painting, deduced from the Laws and Impulses which guide the true Artist in the Production of his Works*.[26] The activity of the reader is genuinely central here, while only nominally central in *Aids to Reflection*. In *Essays on the Principles of Genial Criticism* the reader is initially presented with two quite traditional ("logical") modes of discourse, both supposedly leading to clear understanding and conviction about the nature of the Fine Arts and

25. *Sources, Processes and Methods in Coleridge's Biographia Literaria*, pp. 149–50.

26. I follow the original text in *Felix Farley's Bristol Journal* in five installments, August-September, 1814. The more usual modern text can be found in J. Shawcross's edition of *Biographia Literaria* (London: Oxford University Press, 1907), vol. 2, 219–46. Shawcross's text not only differs widely (and inconsistently) from the original in matters of punctuation, capitalization, and italicization, but seriously misplaces material in the third essay, creating the very confusion about which he complains in notes to his text (vol. 2, 313). See my essay "The Text of Coleridge's *Essays on the Principles of Genial Criticism*," forthcoming in *Modern Philology*.

of the Beautiful. But as the text proceeds, the reader must discard these modes and adopt a more intuitive, self-reflecting and imaginative method of reading and thinking; he must, in short, employ the same "Laws and Impulses which guide the true Artist in the Production of his Works." The experience of "thoughtful" reading *is* the "proof" of the paraphrasable argument of the text. As a dramatic lesson in response to prose, this work, buried away in a provincial newspaper, surpasses *Aids to Reflection* and achieves the originality of the best of the works we have examined in this study. *Essays on the Principles of Genial Criticism* may therefore serve as an appropriate conclusion to our examination of Coleridge and of the role of the reader in romantic prose.

The *Essays* are infinitely more difficult in terms both of aesthetic theory and of rhetoric than the "Preface" of 1796. The Latin epigraph from Giordano Bruno announces the difficulties ahead:

> Unus ergo idemque perpetuo Sol perseverans atque manens aliis atque aliis, aliter atque aliter dispositis, alius efficitur atque alius. Haud secus de hac solari Arte varii varie sentiunt, diversi diversa dicunt: quot capita, tot sententiae — et tot voces. Hinc Corvi crocitant, Cuculi cuculant, Lupi ululant, Sues grundiunt, Oves balant, hinniunt Equi, mugiunt Boves, rudunt Asini. Turpe est, dixit Aristoteles, solicitum esse ad quemlibet interrogantem respondere. Boves Bobus admugiant, Equi Equis adhinniant, Asinis adrudant Asini! Nostrum est Hominibus aliquid circa Hominum excellentissimorum inventiones pertentare.

> (Therefore one and the same sun, while constantly persevering and remaining, yet becomes one thing or another as some objects are disposed some ways sometimes and other objects are disposed other ways at other times. Not unlike this solar manner, various men feel various ways, and different classes of being speak different things: there are as many opinions as heads — and as many voices. Hence crows caw, cuckoos cuckoo, wolves howl, pigs grunt, sheep bleat, horses neigh, cows low, and donkeys bray. Aristotle says it is shame-

ful to be solicitous in answering every one who asks a question. Cows low to cattle, horses neigh to horses, and donkeys bray to donkeys! It is our purpose to prove to men something about the artistic achievements of most excellent men.)

The work will conclude with a Greek quotation of similar emphasis from Plotinus:

"τοῖς μηδέποτε φαντασθεῖσιν, ὡς καλὸν τὸ τῆς δικαιο-
σύνης καὶ σωφροσύνης πρόσωπον, καὶ ὡς οὔτε ἕσπερος
οὔτε ἑῷος οὕτω καλά. Τὸν γὰρ ὁρῶντα πρὸς τὸ ὁρώμε-
νον συγγενὲς καὶ ὅμοιον ποιησάμενον δεῖ ἐπιβάλλειν
τῇ θέᾳ· οὐ γὰρ ἂν πώποτε εἶδεν ὀφθαλμὸς ἥλιον, ἡλιοει-
δὴς μὴ γεγενημένος, οὐδὲ τὸ καλὸν ἂν ἴδοι ψυχὴ μὴ
γενομένη."

(To those to whose imagination it has never been presented, how beautiful is the countenance of justice and wisdom; and that neither the morning nor the evening star are so fair. For in order to direct the view aright, it behoves that the beholder should have made himself congenerous and similar to the object beheld. Never could the eye have beheld the sun, had not its own essence been soliform, [*i.e. pre-configured to light by a similarity of essence with that of light*] neither can a soul not beautiful attain to an intuition of beauty.)[27]

The difference between these two quotations enfolding the three essays and their attached appendix is a difference between negative and positive. The initiating quotation describes the profound limitations of the majority of individuals in achieving an uncluttered perception of truth, in this case, the truth of artistic excellence. The concluding quotation posits the interior disposition or "pre-configuration" needed for that perception. The development of the argument of the enfolded text is, in fact, toward the reader's heightened awareness and activation of his own aesthetic "pre-configuration." Early in *Essays*, Coleridge calls attention to the reader's active participation in the

27. Coleridge's translation, as provided in the sixth chapter of *Biographia Literaria*. See the *Works of Coleridge*, vol. 7, I, 14–15.

discourse. The first "postulate" is that "the reader would steadily look into his own mind to know whether the principles
stated are ideally true." Three paragraphs later Coleridge adds:

> it is in the nature of all disquisitions on matters of taste, that
> the reasoner must appeal for his very premises to facts of
> feeling and of inner sense, which all men do not possess, and
> which many, who do possess and even act upon them, yet
> have never reflectively adverted to, have never made them
> objects of a full and distinct consciousness.

To bring the "facts of feeling and of inner sense" into "full and
distinct consciousness" is the true purpose of these essays.

In order to achieve this, Coleridge in part employs a traditional form of argumentation of apparent conclusiveness: geometric "demonstration"with a preliminary definition and postulates and a concluding scholium. However, imposed on, and
eventually supplanting, this form of "definitive" argumentation
is an allusive, "poetic" structure offering — and requiring — a
more intimate response from the reader than simply following
the connected stages of a logical exposition. Among other devices, Coleridge quotes extended passages of poetry, he con-
structs a dramatic scene in dialogue form, and at climactic
moments he includes — in full Greek capitals — passages of
"mystic" Neoplatonic writing that he acknowledges to be "obscure" but "*tenet umbra Deum*!" Thus, the *structure* and the *rhetoric* of *Essays* ask in part for the operation of the same faculty
that the *theory* of the work posits for true aesthetic perception.
As Coleridge declares in the first essay, "the specific object of
the present attempt is to enable the spectator to judge in the
same spirit in which the Artist produced, or ought to have
produced."

As I have indicated, the "poetic" structure is imposed on
quite traditional modes of exposition and argumentation. The
first essay might be a model of a classical exordium: it attempts
to win a favorable hearing for the topic, by stressing its appropriateness at this time and place, and for the writer, by an-

ticipating the possible objections of the reader as well as by acknowledging Coleridge's own misgivings in embarking on a subject of such "grandeur and delicacy."

Coleridge begins by stating that the "return of peace" — *Essays on the Principles of Genial Criticism* appeared only a few months after Napoleon's exile to Elba — could not be celebrated "more worthily or more appropriately" than by directing "the taste and affections of his readers to the noblest works of Peace." Mindful of his audience in the commercial city of Bristol, he notes that the Fine Arts have a "certain reaction . . . on the more immediate utilities of life" and that they "hold as honorable a rank in our archives of trade, as in those of taste." Regarding his own reservations about handling such a difficult subject, Coleridge reminds the reader of the various collections of painting in Bristol and of a current exhibition by Washington Allston, both of which provide appropriate material for both testing and illustrating the truth of his exposition. In addition to employing these rhetorical tactics, the first essay also begins the geometric discourse with its definition of the "common essence" of all forms of the Fine Arts: "the excitement of emotion for the immediate purpose of pleasure thro' the medium of beauty"; and with two postulates: that "the reader would steadily look into his own mind," and that he should consult the art works mentioned "to judge whether or how far [the principles of the Fine Arts as defined in *Essays* have] been realized."

Despite the initial definition, the postulates, and the scholium later, the text does not in fact fulfill the formal geometric "demonstration" it seems to promise. The very defeat of the expectations that the form initially raises is, I would suggest, another element in Coleridge's strategy to supplant a simple, linear, "logical" process with a more intuitive "poetic" approach. Certainly the start of the second essay takes away the "geometric security." The first sentence draws a distinction between true "mathematical" demonstration, in which definitions are accepted without question, and "philosophic" examinations as offered in these essays, which complete themselves in accurate and proved definitions. Hence, instead of progressing from the definition ("the excitement of emotion for the purpose of immediate pleasure thro' the medium of beauty"), the individual essays look back to it and spend their energy in defending its accuracy.

It is the last phrase of the definition, "thro' the medium of beauty," that occupies the text from the second essay to the end of the series and that both requires and justifies the "poetic" structure. The perception of the beautiful, Coleridge argues, requires "an inner sense," "a regulative principle" not developed in all men and radically different from a passive response to what is "agreeable" either naturally ("that which is congruous with the primary constitution of our senses") or accidentally (by association). The crucial distinction between the beautiful and the agreeable, especially the agreeable by association, is of sufficient importance and difficulty to require extensive development both in the essays and in their summarizing appendix. If the beautiful has no objective "foundation in nature and the noblest faculties of the human mind," Coleridge declares, then "all *rational* enquiry concerning the Arts" is impossible. The activation of those "noblest faculties" through the "poetic" structure is the inevitable procedure of *Essays on the Principles of Genial Criticism*.

In the third essay, following careful distinctions between the two forms of the agreeable, Coleridge offers the first of his several formulations of the beautiful as residing in compositional harmony: "Multeity in Unity," "in which the *many*, still seen as many, becomes *one*." This statement is then further refined by the admission that the naturally agreeable may be a component part of the beautiful: "The result then of the whole is that the shapely (i.e. *formosus*) joined with the *naturally* agreeable, constitutes what speaking accurately we mean by the word beautiful (i.e., *Pulcher*)."

Immediately following this process of definition, Coleridge makes a significant shift in the discussion away from our response to the beautiful simply as residing in sensory compositional harmony. In the first of his direct appeals to the reader's self-reflection, he declares:

> But we are conscious of faculties far superior to the highest impressions of sense: we have life and free-will. — What then will be the result, when the Beautiful arising from regular form is so modified by the perception of life and spontaneous action, as that the latter only shall be the object of our conscious *perception*, while the former merely acts, and yet does effectively act, on our *feelings*?

In the most consummate works of art, the shapely regularity of the "confining FORM" is "*fused* . . . and almost *volatilized* by [FREE LIFE]." Thus, even as he arrives at a satisfactory formal definition, Coleridge advances beyond it by hinting at a still higher functioning of our "inner sense" than the response to form at the center of the refined definition.

The same pattern of refined definition followed by a dramatic intuitive move beyond the definition is found in the extended "recapitulation" of the third essay. Again, the difference between the sensorily or associatedly agreeable and the beautiful is emphasized, and a new formal definition is offered, its "definitiveness" highlighted by italic printing: "*The sense of Beauty subsists in simultaneous intuition of the relation of parts, each to each, and of all to a whole: exciting an immediate and absolute complacency, without intervenience therefore of any interest, sensual or intellectual.*" However, in an elaborate footnote appended to the very beginning of this definition, Coleridge immediately shifts the level of discussion by invoking the Mystics' description of beauty as "the subjection of matter to spirit so as to be transformed into a symbol, in and through which the spirit reveals itself; and declare *that* the *most* beautiful, where the most obstacles to a full manifestation have been most perfectly overcome." (We are in effect asked to consider the topic on two levels — discursive and nondiscursive — at once![28])

28. Shawcross (vol. 2, 239–40) spoils the effect by printing the footnote as a succeeding paragraph.

To describe this higher formulation of the instinct for the beautiful, Coleridge presents a series of exclamatory statements and a quotation — in Greek capitals — of the "obscure" but God-containing Plotinus. Finally, Coleridgean prose turns into Coleridgean poetry as the footnote closes with twenty-eight lines from "Dejection: an Ode." The focus of this nondiscursive elaboration is on a property of the "soul's interior," its own spiritual "purity" being the necessary pre-configuration for the reception of the beautiful, as it seeks kinship and delight from the "spirit" presented to it in the symbols of art:

> Our inmost selves rejoice:
> And thence flows all that glads or ear or sight,
> All melodies the echoes of that voice,
> All colors a suffusion from that light.

The internal movement of *Essays on the Principles of Genial Criticism* is inescapable at this point.

The emphasis on the satisfaction provided by art for the soul's instinct for spiritual beauty leads quite naturally in the scholium to the relation of the beautiful to the good. Despite their obvious differences — the good is "discursive," whereas the beautiful is "intuitive" — the very consideration of the two elements indicates the elevation of the discussion of the beautiful during the course of Coleridge's investigation. Following an imaginary conversation between Milton and "some stern and prejudiced Puritan, contemplating the front of York Cathedral," the essays proper end with the Greek capitals of Plotinus describing the beautiful as the "*calling on* the soul, which receives instantly and welcomes it as something connatural."

The Appendix traverses the entire process of the essays, separating the beautiful from the sensorily or associatedly agreeable, as well as from the perception of means to useful end. Coleridge approaches again the subject of the beautiful and the good, but now emphasizes not their difference but their "relation," as he leaves "the Beauty of the Senses" and the "relatively good" for "the super-sensual Beauty, the Beauty of Vir-

tue and Holiness, and of its relation to the ABSOLUTELY GOOD,
distinguishable, not separable." But "discourse" on this is at
once deferred, as Coleridge waits for "a loftier mood, a nobler
subject, a more appropriate audience." Just as he had to aban-
don conventional discourse increasingly in the course of the
essays, he asserts that it would be "profanation" to attempt to
discuss these "mysteries" in such discourse. Once again, the
text retreats into sacred Greek capitals and the "obscure" but
poetically resonant images of Plotinus that were quoted at the
start of this analysis. The solar image of Bruno's epigraph is repeated in the final words of Plotinus, thus enclosing the essays
in a poetic metaphor. This is quite appropriate to a work that in
its attempt to define the "common essence" of poetry has moved
steadily away from customary exposition into poetry and the attempted activation of the reader's "poetic instinct."

Essays on the Principles of Genial Criticism of 1814, like much
of Coleridge's mature prose, are challenging and difficult as-
signments in reading. They require "thought," that is, "the voluntary re-production in our minds of those states of consciousness to which as to his best and most authentic documents, the
[writer] . . . refers us." In so reading, as Coleridge declares in
Aids to Reflection, "we seek to imitate the artist, while we ourselves make a copy or duplicate of his work."[29] In addition to
shedding some light on the vexed question of Coleridge's pla-
giarisms, this passage is an apt description of the creative kind
of reading to which the best of Coleridge's prose calls us. It is an
apt statement as well of the demands on, and the rewards for,
the reader of romantic prose generally.

In each of the writers surveyed, we are brought into a relationship with the text requiring an exertion of "co-operating
power" that challenges the conventional separations between author and text and reader, between paraphrasable argument and
affective experience, and—perhaps most significantly—between prose criticism and the artistic process itself. It is not ac-

29. "Introductory Aphorisms," footnote to Aphorism viii.

cidental that many of the texts have been concerned with aesthetics or various forms and examples of art: theater, poetry in its varieties ("lyrical ballads," epitaphs, sonnets, and monodies), painting, and architecture. Whether by Lamb, Hazlitt, Wordsworth, or Coleridge, these texts provide "*genial* criticism"; that is, they find their authenticity in the same inner source as the artistic products they describe, the creative capacity of the artist-reader. And even in writings on politics and morals or in Hazlitt's familiar essays, the same grounding of argument in the reader's creative participation prevails. This constitutes the mode and motive of romantic prose in some of its most original manifestations.

BIBLIOGRAPHY

Primary Sources

Ad Herennium. Trans. Harry Caplan. Loeb Classical Library. Cambridge: Harvard University Press; and London: William Heinemann, 1954.

Byron, George Noel Gordon, Lord. *The Works of Lord Byron: with His Letters and Journals and His Life by Thomas Moore*. 17 vols. London, 1832–1833.

Cicero. *De Inventione, De Optimo Genere Oratorum, Topica*. Trans. H. M. Hubbell. Loeb Classical Library. Cambridge: Harvard University Press; and London: William Heinemann, 1976.

Coleridge, Samuel Taylor. *Biographia Literaria*. Ed. J. Shawcross. 2 vols. Oxford: Oxford University Press, 1907.

— — —. *Collected Letters*. Ed. Earl Leslie Griggs. 6 vols. Oxford: Oxford University Press, 1956–1971.

— — —. *Collected Works*. General Editor Kathleen Coburn. Bollingen Series 75. London: Routledge and Kegan Paul; and Princeton: Princeton University Press, 1969–.

— — —. *Complete Poetical Works*. Ed. Ernest Hartley Coleridge. 2 vols. Oxford: Clarendon Press, 1912.

— — —. *Miscellaneous Criticism*. Ed. T. M. Raysor. Cambridge: Harvard University Press, 1936.

— — —. *Notebooks*. Ed. Kathleen Coburn. Bollingen Series 50. London: Routledge and Kegan Paul; and Princeton: Princeton University Press, 1957–.

Delisle, Fanny. *A Study of Shelley's "A Defence of Poetry": A Textual and Critical Evaluation*. 2 vols. Salzburg Studies in English Literature, Romantic Reassessment 27–28. Salzburg, 1974.

129

De Quincey, Thomas. *Selected Essays on Rhetoric*. Ed. Frederick Burwick. Carbondale and Edwardsville: Southern Illinois University Press, 1967.

Enfield, William. "Is Verse Essential to Poetry?" *Monthly Magazine* 2 (1976): 453–56.

Hazlitt, William. *Complete Works*. Ed. P. P. Howe. 21 vols. London and Toronto: J. M. Dent, 1930–1934.

Hunt, Leigh. *Autobiography*. Ed. J. E. Morpurgo. London: Cresset Press, 1949.

Johnson, Samuel. *Works*. Ed. Arthur Murphy. 12 vols. London, 1801.

— — —. *Yale Edition of the Works of Samuel Johnson*. General Editors Allen Hazen and John Middendorf. New Haven and London: Yale University Press, 1958 — .

Lamb, Charles. *Letters of Charles and Mary Anne Lamb*. Ed. Edwin W. Marrs, Jr. Ithaca: Cornell University Press, 1975 — .

— — —. *Works of Charles and Mary Lamb*. Ed. E. V. Lucas. 7 vols. London: Methuen and Company, 1903–1905.

Quintilian. *The Institutio Oratoria*. Trans. H. E. Butler. 4 vols. Loeb Classical Library. Cambridge: Harvard University Press; and London: William Heinemann, 1966–1968.

Shelley, Percy Bysshe. *Letters*. Ed. Frederick L. Jones. 2 vols. Oxford: Oxford University Press, 1964.

The Spectator. Ed. Donald F. Bond. 5 vols. Oxford: Oxford University Press, 1965.

Wordsworth, William. *The Letters of William and Dorothy Wordsworth: The Early Years 1787–1805*. Ed. Ernest de Selincourt. 2d ed. revised by Chester L. Shaver. Oxford: Oxford University Press, 1967.

— — —. *The Letters of William and Dorothy Wordsworth: The Middle Years*. Ed. Ernest de Selincourt. Revised by Mary Moorman and Alan G. Hall. 2 vols. Oxford University Press, 1969–1970.

— — —. *The Letters of William and Dorothy Wordsworth: The Later Years*. Ed. Ernest de Selincourt. 3 vols. Oxford: Oxford University Press, 1939.

— — —. *Literary Criticism*. Ed. Paul M. Zall, Lincoln: University of Nebraska Press, 1966.

— — —. *Prose Works*. Ed. W. J. B. Owen and Jane Worthington Smyser. 3 vols. Oxford: Oxford University Press, 1974.

Secondary Sources

Aarsleff, Hans. "Wordsworth, Language, and Romanticism." *Essays in Criticism* 30 (1980): 215–26.

Abrams, M. H. *The Mirror and the Lamp*. New York: Oxford University Press, 1953.

Albrecht, W. P. *Hazlitt and the Creative Imagination*. Lawrence: University of Kansas Press, 1965.

— — —. "Structure in Two of Hazlitt's Essays." *Studies in Romanticism* 21 (1982): 181–90.

Berlin, James A. "The Rhetoric of Romanticism: The Case for Coleridge." *Rhetoric Society Quarterly* 10 (1980): 62–74.

Bialostosky, Don H. "Coleridge's Interpretation of Wordsworth's Preface to *Lyrical Ballads*." *PMLA* 93 (1978): 912–24.

Bromwich, David. *Hazlitt: The Mind of a Critic*. New York: Oxford University Press, 1983.

Christensen, Jerome. *Coleridge's Blessed Machine of Language*. Ithaca: Cornell University Press, 1981.

Cooke, M. G. "*Quisque Sui Faber:* Coleridge in the *Biographia Literaria*." *Philological Quarterly* 50 (1971): 208–229.

Frank, Robert D. *Don't Call Me Gentle Charles!* Corvallis: Oregon State University Press, 1976.

Friedman, Michael H. *The Making of a Tory Humanist*. New York: Columbia University Press, 1979.

Hanson, Lawrence. *The Life of S. T. Coleridge: The Early Years*. London: Oxford University Press, 1938.

Harding, Anthony John. "Coleridge's College Declamation, 1792." *The Wordsworth Circle* 8 (1977): 361–67.

Haven, Richard. "The Romantic Art of Charles Lamb." *ELH* 30 (1963): 137–46.

Hayden, John O. *The Romantic Reviewers 1802–1824*. London: Routledge and Kegan Paul, 1969.

The Hazlitts: An Account of their Origin and Descent. W. Carew Hazlitt, ed. Edinburgh: Ballantyne, Hanson and Co., 1911.

Heffernan, James A. W. *Wordsworth's Theory of Poetry: The Transforming Imagination*. Ithaca: Cornell University Press, 1969.

Hunt, Jr., Bishop C. "Coleridge and the Endeavour of Philosophy." *PMLA* 91 (1976): 829–39.

Kinnaird, John. *William Hazlitt: Critic of Power*. New York: Columbia University Press, 1978.

Law, Marie H. *The English Familiar Essay in the Early Nineteenth Century*. Philadelphia: University of Pennsylvania, 1934.

Mallette, R. "Narrative Technique in the *Biographia Literaria*." *Modern Language Review* 70 (1975): 32–40.

Merritt, Travis R. "Taste, Opinion, and Theory in the Rise of Victorian Prose Stylism." In *The Art of Victorian Prose*, ed. George Levine and William Madden. New York: Oxford University Press, 1968.

Monsman, Gerald. *Confessions of a Prosaic Dreamer: Charles Lamb's Art of Autobiography*. Durham, N.C.: Duke University Press, 1984.

Mulcahy, Daniel J. "Charles Lamb: The Antithetical Manner and the Two Planes." *Studies in English Literature* 3 (1963): 517–42.

Nabholtz, John R. "Drama and Rhetoric in Lamb's Essays of the Imagination." *Studies in English Literature* 12 (1972): 683–703.

———. "Modes of Discourse in Hazlitt's Prose." *The Wordsworth Circle* 10 (1979): 97–106.

— — —. "Romantic Prose and Classical Rhetoric." *The Wordsworth Circle* 11 (1980): 119–26.

Randel, Fred V. *The World of Elia: Charles Lamb's Essayistic Romanticism*. Port Washington, N.Y.: Kennikat Press, 1975.

Ready, Robert. *Hazlitt at Table*. Rutherford, N.J.: Fairleigh Dickinson University Press, 1981.

Reiman, Donald H. "Thematic Unity in Lamb's Familiar Essays." *JEGP* 64 (1965): 470–78.

Sanderson, David R. "Coleridge's Political 'Sermons': Discursive Language and the Voice of God." *Modern Philology* 70 (1973): 319–30.

— — —. "Wordsworth's World, 1809: A Stylistic Study of the Cintra Pamphlet." *The Wordsworth Circle* 1 (1970): 104–13.

Scoggins, James O. "Images of Eden in the Essays of Elia." *JEGP* 71 (1972): 198–210.

— — —. "The Preface to *Lyrical Ballads*: A Revolution in Dispute." In *Studies in Criticism and Aesthetics, 1600–1800*, ed. Howard Anderson and John S. Shea. Minneapolis: University of Minnesota Press, 1967.

Wallace, G. M. *The Design of Biographia Literaria*. Winchester, Mass.: Allen and Unwin, 1983.

Watson, Melvin R. *Magazine Serials and the Essay-Tradition, 1746–1820*. Louisiana State University Studies, Humanities Series, 6. Baton Rouge: Louisiana State University Press, 1956.

Wimsatt, W. K., Jr. *The Prose Style of Samuel Johnson*. New Haven: Yale University Press, 1941.

Wheeler, Kathleen M. *Sources, Processes and Methods in Coleridge's Biographia Literaria*. Cambridge: Cambridge University Press, 1980.

Wordsworth, Christopher. *Scholae Academicae: Some Account of the Studies at the English Universities in the Eighteenth Century*. Cambridge: Cambridge University Press, 1910.